Maury County Remembered

Maury County Remembered

The Gilbert MacWilliams Orr Collection

Compiled and Edited by

Lois Harlan Orr and Gilbert MacWilliams Orr Jr.

HILLSBORO PRESS
Franklin, Tennessee

TENNESSEE HERITAGE LIBRARY
Bicentennial Collection

Printed in the United States of America

03   02   01   00   99   1   2   3   4   5

Library of Congress Catalog Card Number: 99–67601

ISBN: 1–57736–164–4

Cover design by Gary Bozeman

Published by
HILLSBORO PRESS
An imprint of
PROVIDENCE HOUSE PUBLISHERS
238 Seaboard Lane • Franklin, Tennessee 37067
800-321-5692
www.providencehouse.com

To
the memory of
Gilbert MacWilliams Orr
1892–1949

"NEIGHBORS FOR NINETY YEARS"

First Farmers & Merchants National Bank and Maury County

THE PEOPLE OF MAURY COUNTY HAVE CREATED AN EVENTFUL HISTORY—SOMETIMES difficult, more often triumphant—and have always moved forward with hope, faith, and determination.

In 1909 a group of neighbors in Mt. Pleasant created a piece of that history by establishing the Farmers & Merchants Bank. They dedicated the bank to community service and set to work. After weathering the Great Depression, First Farmers & Merchants began a steady pattern of growth, expansion, and innovation. In 1940 the first branch office was opened in Spring Hill. The headquarters was moved to Columbia in 1950. The bank's national charter was received in 1954. The 1985 purchase of the Bank of Loretto began a geographic expansion that now extends to five midstate counties. The Trust Department exceeded the billion-dollar mark in 1994, and in 1996, the bank grew to $500 million in assets.

Through the years we have worked with our neighbors to build a strong and vibrant community. Today Maury County is emerging as the commercial, industrial, agricultural, educational, medical, and financial capital of southern Middle Tennessee. At the heart of that development is First Farmers & Merchants National Bank—Tennessee's leading independent community bank.

In 1999, First Farmers & Merchants National Bank and Maury County have been "Neighbors for Ninety Years." To celebrate that anniversary First Farmers & Merchants is pleased to help present *Maury County Remembered*, and we are grateful to the Orr family for sharing their reflection on our community's colorful past.

Waymon L. Hickman

Waymon L. Hickman
Chairman and CEO

Waymon L. Hickman   *T. Randy Stevens*   *Virgil H. Moore Jr.*
Chairman and CEO   *President and COO*   *Senior Chairman*

CONTENTS

Foreword

    Gilbert MacWilliams Orr (1892–1949)

        by Houston Gray   ix

Preface and Acknowledgments   xvii

1. The Dimple of the Universe   3

2. Columbia—The County Seat   21

3. Historic Homes   43

4. Farm Scenes   83

5. Horses and Horse Shows   119

6. Mules and Mule Day Festivities   139

Afterword

    "Things I Love"

        by Gilbert MacWilliams Orr   167

Index   171

FOREWORD

Gilbert MacWilliams Orr
1892–1949
by Houston Gray

Beneath a clear, blue Tennessee sky, surrounded by the things he loved and the people who loved him, the mortal remains of Gilbert MacWilliams Orr were laid to their final "rest in sweet oblivion."

Death, as it must to all men, had come to Gillie Orr at his home in Columbia, Tennessee, on the afternoon of May 10, 1949, as he was preparing, typically, to attend a meeting of horsemen. As the news of his sudden death became widespread, a shocked world of friends and acquaintances tried to reconcile itself to its loss.

Those friends find it difficult to conceive of a world without his presence. It is hard to adjust to the sad fact that we will no longer hear his cheerful voice announcing horse shows; that we can no longer read the latest breezy news of horses and men from his facile pen. Worse still, none can experience again that feeling of inner warmth resulting from even a short conversation with the splendid personality who gave so freely of his real love for his fellow man.

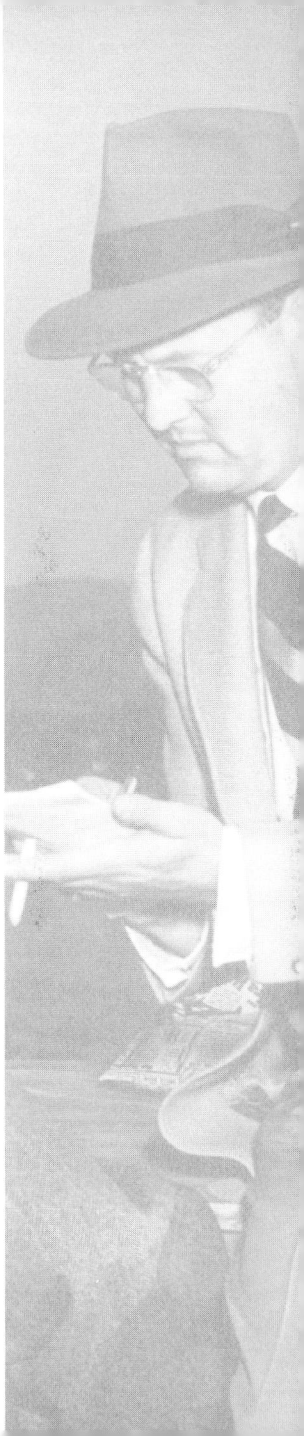

It is difficult to envision Gillie Orr without being keenly conscious of his great love of life, in spite of the frequent cruel blows it had struck him. He of the great heart has left the imprint of his influence on all who knew him. When he asked, "How are you getting along?" it was no mere casual greeting. He was truly interested in the welfare of mankind,

and from the obvious sincerity of the cordial salutation, you knew he really hoped you were getting along well. To have met Gillie Orr and enjoyed his gracious, affable charm was a happy occasion. It was a superb experience to have known him and had the opportunity to bask in the radiance of his genuine sincerity.

Inspiration of lesser men, greatness rested lightly on the heavily burdened shoulders of this man who gave so much to friendship. His was the greatness of heart and spirit; of a courage able to face trials and hurts heavier than most men are called on to bear. His was the greatness that rose above the anguish of the body to spread sincere "good will toward men."

The son of Billy Mac and Sarah Gilbert Orr, Gilbert MacWilliams Orr was born October 28, 1892, in Prospect, Giles County, Tennessee. As a boy he moved to Columbia, where he attended the public schools, but his summers until he reached the age of sixteen were spent on the Giles County farms of his two grandfathers, and there he gained his early love for horses and the country life.

Well educated, well traveled, and the friend of myriads of people of high and low station throughout the United States, at heart he remained a country boy from Middle Tennessee who truly loved all that country living represents. His writings reflected his inherent love of the outdoors as exemplified by pastoral sights, sounds, and odors. Sophisticates enjoyed him for the simplicity and beauty of his articles on subjects close to the soil, while old-timers laughed with him at the memories he evoked of life in rural Tennessee in "the good old days."

After graduating from Central High School in Columbia, he entered the University of the South at Sewanee, Tennessee, where he was initiated into Kappa Alpha fraternity and became manager of the football team, a member of the debating team, and president of the German Dance Club.

Then, at the end of his junior year at college, this happy, attractive, popular young man suffered his first major tragedy when he was cut down by the relentless crippler, poliomyelitis. What hope for a bright young man, convalescing from such a long, serious, debilitating illness? What future for a light-hearted youth whose way of life had so suddenly been altered? No more "Germans!" No more walking across a football field with the team after a game, to speak words of encouragement after a loss and congratulations after a winning game. A dismal future apparently faced this fine young man with the weakened legs.

But, with that valor understood so well by those who knew him, Gillie Orr rose to surmount these terrifying new circumstances, and determined to train himself for a legal career. When his health permitted, he entered Cumberland University at Lebanon, Tennessee, where he received his law degree, and later passed the State of Tennessee bar examinations.

NEW FIELDS OF ENDEAVOR

Back in Columbia, he hung out his new shingle and started practicing his new-found profession. After the usual period of struggle through which young lawyers go, he began to realize that the cold impersonality of the law could not be reconciled with the warmth of his feeling for people, and he determined to find some less inhibiting field of endeavor. At that time he was serving as a Magistrate in the Maury County Quarterly Court, so, in 1922, he ran for the office of County Court Clerk, and was elected, serving three consecutive terms in office.

On December 17, 1927, Miss Virginia Street of Alexander City, Alabama, became Mrs. Gilbert MacWilliams Orr. Leaving the law and politics, the Orrs set out to travel around the South producing amateur plays for civic clubs and community groups in Alabama, Tennessee, North Carolina, and Kentucky. Meeting new people, arranging costumes, writing publicity, watching amateur actors learning their lines, seeing new places and moving on, was a satisfying way of living that appealed to

WSM Radio, Gilbert M. Orr at left.

The Gilbert MacWilliams Orr Collection

Jack Knox—*"So long Old Timer, we'll be missing you tremendously."*

this man to whom people meant so much. This good life made up for a lot of those brooding sickbed thoughts, and those thwarting incidents when it was so hard to rationalize justice and the law.

Gilbert MacWilliams Orr Jr. first saw the light of day on May 6, 1936. A son—a fine, strapping baby boy! This, too, helped compensate for so many of those dark, empty, cheerless days of youth, when illness held the upper hand, and hope lay quiescent. A son to bear the name, the hopes, the dreams! But, once more tragedy struck its deadly blow, and, four days later, on May 10, Mrs. Orr died. The man of good cheer was once more faced with what seemed to be more than human spirit could endure.

ENTER THE TENNESSEE WALKING HORSE

A little later, almost by accident, Gillie Orr became professionally interested in Tennessee Walking Horses. One spring day in 1938 he drove to Lewisburg, Tennessee, where he understood that a well-known Jersey cattle man was staging an auction sale of Tennessee Walking Horses. He had heard of Jimmy Joe Murray and he knew of Tennessee Walking Horses, but an auction sale of this little-known breed was something he wanted to know more about. He witnessed the first of what later became the famous Murray Farm Sale. He saw Jimmy Joe Murray on the rostrum praising this breed of horse and exhorting buyers to raise their bids. He heard Auctioneer Jim McCord, later Congressman from Tennessee and still later governor of that state, chant the prices in an effort to get the bids increased. From that day, Gillie was a devotee of the Tennessee Walking Horse, and from that day dates the beginning of his new career devoted to the horse of the free and easy gaits.

Lives there the man who knows Tennessee Walking Horses who has not heard of Gilbert M. Orr? From that start in 1938, Gillie Orr carved out for himself a place in the Tennessee Walking Horse world that can never be taken by any one man. On his death the question arose, "Who can take Gillie's place?" No one can take Gillie's place, because Gillie did not hold a *job* for which some younger man had been trained, or to which some experienced man could hope to succeed. He had made for himself a *career*—one so broad in its scope that many will have to be called to try to fill even parts of his work. He was "Mr. Tennessee Walking Horse" to people from all parts of the country. Announcer, promoter, editor, author, manager, columnist, advertising man—these were his contribution to the Tennessee Walking Horse that all the world knew. Advisor, counsellor, trouble-shooter and peacemaker—these hidden characteristics of the man were known more by horsemen than by the outside world.

Of columnists, editors, advertising men, announcers, authors, horse show managers, and lovers of the Tennesse Walking Horse there are many. Who among them can combine all of these characteristics as did Gillie Orr? None, since only he had that talent to handle successfully all of these jobs—plus the charm and personality of a man who loved people, who attracted people, and who held their complete confidence.

Cover of 1949's The Blue Ribbon, *Official Year Book of the Eleventh Annual Tennessee Walking Horse National Celebration.*

To list his contributions to the Tennessee Walking Horse is needless, since all who knew him know also of what he has done for the breed.

From that beginning, Gillie Orr went on singing the praises of the Tennessee Walking Horse. In May, 1939, he started his well-known column, "Speaking of Horses" in the *Nashville Banner*. That same spring he covered his first horse show for the paper at Franklin, Tennessee, and in September of that year, the *Banner* sent him to Shelbyville, Tennessee, to cover a horse show.

CELEBRATION ACTIVITIES

It was called, somewhat presumptuously perhaps, the First Annual Tennessee Walking Horse National Celebration. It was the first big horse show to feature Tennessee Walking Horses, and a most ambitious undertaking at that time. It was the joint effort of a group of civic-minded Shelbyville men and a like group of ardent Tennessee Walking Horse enthusiasts. At that time many cities throughout Tennessee were starting annual celebrations or festivals, but few have survived the years, and many of those which did survive, have not been continuous. Gillie Orr was a major factor in the growth of the Celebration and in its continuous existence for eleven consecutive years. [Note: As *Maury County Remembered* goes to press, the 1999 Celebration is underway making that *sixty-one* consecutive years.]

The following year Gilbert M. Orr first contributed to THE BLUE RIBBON, and was made Director-General of the

Celebration. From 1941 until his death, he continued as both Director–General and Editor of THE BLUE RIBBON, having taken on the latter job the year following. As editor, he has written much of the material, but also had the imagination and ingenuity to collect a wide assortment of interesting horse stories for the book.

ANNOUNCER EXTRAORDINAIRE

At the 1940 Celebration, Gillie first essayed to act as master of ceremonies at a big horse show. His early realization of his own shortcomings along these lines was the foundation of his brilliant success as the most sought after horse show announcer in the South. Never satisfied with his own announcing, he asked constructive criticism of his friends, and studied the problem of accoustics, microphone technique, good timing, and general horse show procedure. He knew that the public liked a fast-moving horse show, and developed a remarkable skill in filling in unavoidable dead spots with his ready wit and his ability to project his charm and enthusiasm over the mechanical, often squawling, speaking system.

Always in demand as an announcer, he seldom refused requests for his services except for previous commitments. He had announced horse shows at Madison Square Garden, New York City, and the Coliseum in Chicago, and at the same time, rarely failed to appear at a small community one-nighter if he weren't otherwise booked. Hardly a horse show patron in the South has failed to hear his smooth-flowing, "Good evening ladies and gentlemen," as another night of classes opened, and his famous, "Rack On!" reflected his own sincere delight at seeing a class of five-gaited beauties at the fast gait. Always a lover of the road horse, his "Let 'em go!" had brought countless thousands to their feet as the trotters opened up and "poured on the coal." "Let your horses CAN-ter, please," was his distinctive way of notifying riders to change to the easy, rolling gait.

Beside being editor of THE BLUE RIBBON, and conducting his weekly newspaper column, Gillie Orr handled all advertising and publicity for the Tennessee Walking Horse Breeders' Association of America, Lewisburg, Tennessee. He has written hundreds of ads for that group, and was responsible for the attractive booklet it publishes on the Tennessee Walking Horse. He was also Tennessee Walking Horse editor for *Saddle and Bridle* magazine, and had contributed to more horse publications than he could remember. In his own estimate, he had "contributed stories galore on the Tennessee Walking Horse to publications all over the country," and was "never happier than when telling the world about this breed of the light horse which is indigenous to Tennessee." He knew hundreds of breeders throughout the country, and was ever ready to help them with a good word for their breed.

He had served as general manager for the annual Mule Day at Columbia a good many times, and had also served as temporary secretary of the Columbia Chamber of Commerce. He was manager of the annual Kiwanis Club horse show in that city, and was a member of that civic organization. He was one of the organizers of, and an active member of the Maury County Horsemen's Association, and had done Boy Scout and other civic work in his home city.

He is survived by his son, known throughout the horse world as *Gillie Mac*, and his sister, Miss Mary Phillips Orr of Columbia. Such was the greatness of the man, however, that his legion of friends, admirers, and acquaintances also feel themselves survivors in the broad sense. Loved by rich and poor, perhaps the greatest tribute of all was contained in a wire of condolence received the day after his death. It came from an obscure waiter in a hotel far removed from Columbia, where Gillie Orr had frequently stopped for meals on his travels. To a bereaved family, this appreciative waiter telegraphed, "Your loss is my loss, for I have lost a friend."

FRIEND,—Requiescat!

Reprinted from *The Blue Ribbon* (1949), the Official Year Book of the Tennessee Walking Horse National Celebration.

PREFACE AND ACKNOWLEDGMENTS

Gilbert MacWilliams Orr left behind a treasure trove of memories which he valued enough to carefully preserve for future generations. Cleaning out the family attic was our first project after retiring. It was not until then that we realized Mr. Orr literally had kept rooms full of memorabilia including the material for this book, *Maury County Remembered*. These photographs and articles had been preserved fifty years in the attic undisturbed. The top of the container for the photographs was labeled:

Very Valuable—Do-not-destroy.

The manuscripts were preserved in a notebook.

These visual and written images from over half a century ago awaken us to the past in Maury County. They record the passing of a way of life; the livelihoods, styles, and customs which grow fainter with each passing day.

We love to look over old photographs as connections with a time which seems almost unrecognizable to us now. Former scenes of rural and small-town life—churches, schools, homes, industries, farms, Mule Days, and horse shows—are a photographic retrospective which hopes to promote a warm view of the past and to preserve a portion of Maury County. We have kept Mr. Orr's journalistic style and his exact language which is representative of mid-twentieth century culture. The images seem to belong to an era some have forgotten and of course most never knew. *Maury County Remembered*, in these long-ago photographs and words by Gilbert MacWilliams Orr, gives each of us an appreciation of the past and a legacy for the new millennium.

We gratefully acknowledge the significant contributions of the following: First Farmers & Merchants National Bank—especially Waymon L. Hickman and Paul T. Butts Jr. who believed in this project; and Andrew B. Miller and his creative, skilled staff at Providence House Publishers for their genuine interest in our family's historical archives.

With best wishes to Gilbert MacWilliams Orr— a man who really knows his jackass! F.C. Sowell WLAC

WLAC Radio. F. C. Sowell and Gilbert M. Orr.

MAURY COUNTY REMEMBERED

Maury County Remembered

THE DIMPLE
OF THE UNIVERSE

Maury County, chanted and related in song and story as "The Dimple of the Universe," is in the bluegrass section of Middle Tennessee, and in that portion of the South where four distinct seasons rotate with such gentle change that one is hardly aware of their passing except to note the warmth of the sunshine in summer and the pleasant penetration of the cold in winter, and to revel in the verdant beauty of spring and the golden loveliness of fall.

Endowed with the natural growth of bluegrass and adorned with a varied species of trees, the eye may feast upon pastoral vistas which are accentuated by streams from over-flowing springs and a river that winds its way through the heart of the county whose soil is as fertile as any upon the face of a beneficent earth.

Broad, smooth highways pass estates on which colonial mansions have stood since the days when Tennessee was young in the sisterhood of states. The atmosphere of the old South still exists in some types of architecture and in the hospitality of the people; but modern progress is evident in scientific farming and diversification of crops, in the physical aspect of good roads and prosperous towns, and in the economic advantages which are second to none in any section of America.

Located in the Tennessee Valley, in the northwest corner of the area of the TVA, Maury County has a large portion of its land within that limited region where the soil of the Tennessee watershed is as productive as any in the nation. This is true because this soil was formed from underlying rocks rich in mineral plant foods, especially phosphate and lime.

Here one finds lands in thick sodded pastures where farming has been carried on for generations without the necessity of artificial fertilization. The livestock industry flourishes in this county which is conducive to its normal and natural pursuit. Winter cover crops enable the farmer to carry his cattle and sheep through the winter season without the necessity of grain-feeding.

Primarily agricultural, Maury County enjoys a growing season of approximately 200 days. All small grains are grown; wheat, oats, hay, irish and sweet potatoes are produced; white burley tobacco is a highly profitable agriultural commodity; and corn is cultivated and harvested in large abundance. All vegetables of the temperate zone are grown here, while peaches, apples, and pears are the principal fruits. This section is justly famous for its berries and melons. Poultry affords a vast income to farmers.

Cattle, sheep, and hogs are the chief animals of the livestock industry. Maury County lambs often bring a premium on the market. Milk cows furnish a steady source of revenue to

Maury County farmland, 1940s.

dwellers on the farm, and thousands of Jersey cows here are high producers of butter fat. Mules are a commercial commodity and are produced in such large number that this county has become the center of an industry that mounts into five figures on the market annually. The famous Tennessee Walking Horse abounds here and is in high demand throughout the year.

Maury County has many trees on many gently rolling hills, and much bluegrass in lush green valleys.

It is as a place of residence that this region makes a strong appeal to those who enjoy richness of life along with security. Congenial neighbors make for happier living here where the best traditions of the South have been kept alive by succeeding generations—not in a fixed or static manner, but leavened with the highest standards of the new day and the age gone by.

The greatest assets of Columbia and Maury County are the men and women who constitute the citizenship, a people who cherish social and cultural standards that build for substance in life. Not only are they essentially substantial, but they are hospitable, genteel, and progressive—"good neighbors" all. Strangers admire them on first acquaintance, and find friendships easily cultivated through association.

Once a resident here, no matter where you may later roam, never will you find atmosphere more alluring or environment more stimulating of the desire "to live and die in Columbia" . . . in Maury County, Tennessee . . . in "The Dimple of the Universe."

HISTORY

Maury County, Tennessee, was formed November 24, 1807 from a part of Williamson County. It was named in honor of Major Abram P. Maury—(pronounced "Murray")—a distinguished soldier who later served under General Andrew Jackson in the War of 1812.

Cattle resting in the shade.

Most of the early settlers of this area were Revolutionary soldiers and their descendants, who came from Virginia and the Carolinas across the mountains to their new homes in the wilderness. Today the Anglo-Saxon strain predominates so exclusively that only .11% of the total population is foreign-born.

A Tennessee Walking Horse colt.

One of the first acts of the settlers in Maury County was the building of a church, which also served as a schoolhouse. The minister, the Rev. William A. Henderson, was likewise the teacher—among his pupils was James Knox Polk, later to become the eleventh President of the United States. The ancestral home of Polk is preserved today and is a shrine in Columbia where thousands of tourists visit it annually.

Columbia was chosen as the County Seat one year after the county was organized, and on December 21, 1808, the County Court held its first session in this city which was incorporated in the year 1817.

Since its foundation, Maury County has enjoyed a rather even-flowing history. While the War between the States caused an interruption of its progress for a time, the county did not suffer markedly from any extensive conflicts within its borders.

Within recent times Maury County has become increasingly important from industrial development and as a center for the production and sale of mules, and for the production of brown phosphate rock and its attendant by-products.

EDUCATION

Public education in Maury County, including all incorporated towns, is furnished exclusively by the county.

The investment in buildings, grounds, and equipment is $500,00 with a per capita investment of around $80 against about $50 for the state average of all counties.

There are at present 72 elementary schools and 8 high schools serving an average scholastic population of approximately 7,000 pupils, of which number about 5,000 are white and 2,000 are colored. There are 162 white teachers and 52 colored teachers constituting the faculties of the schools. Of the eight high schools, six are for white pupils and two are for colored pupils.

An average number of around 1,200 pupils are transported daily to and from the public schools in 30 county-owned buses at a cost of approximately $8.90 per pupil per school year.

CLIMATE

In general, the climate in Columbia and Maury County is mild with relatively short and broken winters. The average annual precipitation is approximately 47 inches which is well distributed throughout the year.

The average annual snowfall is only 7 inches, and occurs chiefly during December, January, and February. Snows here last but for a day or two; seldom are they longer in melting away.

The average annual temperature for Columbia and Maury County is 59.2 degrees F. The annual range of temperature is from 40.1 degrees in January to 78.1 degrees in July. The average monthly temperature is 75.4 degrees during June, July, August, and September.

AGRICULTURE

Approximately half the population of Maury County is rural. On the farms of this county 50.91% of its people dwell. More than 50% of the farms are operated by the owners.

Maury County has an area of 582 square miles and is from 600 to 700 feet above sea level. Its area contains

372,480 acres, of which number 351,105 acres, or 94.3% of the whole, are in farm lands—of this percentage, 59% of the area is in improved lands. There are 4,419 farms in the county which are valued at $10,000,000 with an average of 79 acres per farm.

Products produced on the farms of Maury County are valued at slightly more than $4,000,000 per annum.

HIGHWAYS AND MOTOR VEHICLES

Two United States Highways traversing Maury County from North to South, and intersecting with State Highways from East to West at Columbia, connect this section with all points of the country.

Approximately 1,000 miles of roads are included in the public highways system of Maury County—all roads lead to and through Columbia, the county seat which is in the center of the county. It is estimated that 700 miles of the highway system in this county are of all-weather type roads.

More than 7,000 motor vehicles are registered in Maury County; of this number, approximately 6,000 are passenger cars and the remainder are of the commercial type.

RAILWAYS, TELEPHONE, AND TELEGRAPH COMMUNICATION

Columbia is on the Cincinnati-to-New Orleans line of the Louisville & Nashville Railroad Company, being a part of the Birmingham Division. It is the terminal point of the Nashville, Florence & Sheffield Division of the L & N to Muscle Shoals and Wilson Dam; it is the terminus of the

Columbia Division of the Nashville, Chattanooga & St. Louis Railway.

Columbia, and other parts of the county as well, is served by the Western Union and Postal Telegraph and Cable Companies for telegraphic communication.

The Southern Bell Telephone Company has central exchanges in Columbia and Mt. Pleasant, and local exchanges in Spring Hill, Culleoka, Sante Fe, Hampshire, Williamsport, and Southport. The county has more than 3,000 telephones in use, and several local exchanges are being switched over to the dial system.

TAXATION AND GOVERNMENT

The assessed valuation of all property in Maury County is in excess of $18,000,000—slightly less than one-third of this amount is for property in the city of Columbia.

The rate of taxation, both for the State and County and for the City of Columbia, is around $1.50 as an average over a period of years. The rate of $1.50 being per hundred dollar valuation; and this is against about $2.25 for all counties of Tennessee in general.

Maury County has no net bonded indebtedness.

As an insight into the business management of the county, the following figures of per capita items are of interest to show the healthy state of finances here: (The first figures are for Maury County, and the second are for the state average of all counties in Tennessee)—

Receipts $11.00 against $12.00

Governmental cost $8.90 against $9.90

Interest $0.15 against $1.50

Capital outlays $0.06 against $1.40

Expenditures $9.00 against $12.00

Surplus $1.90 against a deficit of $0.50

Bond amortization requirement $0.20 against $1.50

In the county government, the County Judge is the fiscal agent of the county; the legislative body is a Quarterly County Court composed of 24 Magistrates, one from the county seat, one from each incorporated town, and two from each of the ten civil districts.

The aldermanic form of government prevails for the city of Columbia—a mayor and two alderman from each of the five city wards.

WHOLESALE AND RETAIL BUSINESS

About 40 wholesale firms do an annual business, chiefly in Columbia, of slightly more than $4,000,000 per year in net sales, and have annual payrolls of approximately $100,000.

In the retail field of business 300 stores have net sales per year of about $8,250,000 and pay their employees around $600,000 annually.

Service industries have 160 establishments with receipts of about $300,000 per annum with a payroll of $60,000 yearly.

MANUFACTURING

The total value of manufactured products in Columbia and Maury County amounts to approximately $9,000,000 per year; and the total payroll from these plants in this city and county approximates the sum of $3,000,000 annually.

ABOVE
W. M. Dean Marble Company.

RIGHT
Drag line loading phosphate dirt.

Manufacturing is confined chiefly to phosphatic materials, chemicals, fertilizers, fabrics, hosiery, food stuffs, and lumber.

Of the above, the phosphatic industry accounts for approximately two-thirds of the totals, both in value of products and in payrolls.

Monsanto Chemical Company and Victor Chemical Works have plants in Maury County which manufacture elemental phosphorous as a base for phosphoric acid. These plants were recently erected at a cost in excess of $5,000,000—employing a great number of men, their annual payrolls are large.

To this must be added the vast holdings of phosphate lands by the Tennessee Valley Authority in Maury County.

With further reports from Monsanto and Victor, and with the expansion of the TVA interests, Maury County's production of phosphate rock and phosphatic materials is reasonably expected to substantially increase both in tonnage and in value by dollars.

Maury County's production of phosphate rock in 1937 constituted 98.07 of the total for Tennessee. Figures for 1938 are not as yet available, but production here is definitely on the increase with all plants running full-force and full-time.

MINERAL RESOURCES

The production of brown phosphate rock and phosphatic materials constitutes, chiefly, the commercial mineral resources of Maury County. Its production amounts to more than $5,500,000 annually. More than 1,500 persons are employed in this vast industry which has a payroll of approximately $1,750,000 per year.

The largest companies mining brown phosphate rock are the Charleston Mining & Manufacturing Company, International Agricultural Corporation, Armour Fertilizer Works, Hoover & Mason and Federal Chemical Company.

MINING AND PROCESSING

Phosphate rock is taken from the vast deposits in Maury County by the open-mining method, the deposits being near the surface of the ground. It is dug with drag-lines equipped with bucket, cable, and boom. From the mines to the plants it is hauled in tramcars and dumped for washing and drying. The dried rock is ground in some plants here,

Monsanto Chemical Company in the early years.

but for the most part is shipped for further processing into fertilizer and other by-products.

When phosphate was first discovered it was dug by hand and only the large lumps of the rock were taken from the mines. For many years the main demand was for rock containing 70 to 78 per cent BPL; however, at the present time, due to improved methods of washing and separating the fine sizes from the impurities, not only are vast deposits of low-grade phosphate rock being successfully concentrated by flotation (a method of reclaiming minute particles of rock by the use of fish oil), but old dump heaps are being reworked. The material discarded by the past generation is being recovered and used by the present generation. Moreover, the calcine process (treatment with heat) has made possible the mining and use of phosphatic matrix without the necessity of separating the rock from impurities.

The figures given above include the price of matrix which consists of lump rock phosphate, phosphate sand, clay, and muck–the latter being a mixture of phosphatic material and clay.

CARBON PRODUCTS

The National Carbon Company, which has just completed its newest manufacturing plant at Columbia, Tennessee, is a

Hauling phosphate dirt to process into phosphorus.

pioneer in the production of carbon and allied products. First organized in 1886, it traces its origin to the demand for arc light carbons following the commercial introduction of the electric arc lamp for public illumination.

From this beginning, the National Carbon Company has continued to expand its interests until today it requires the facilities of ten primary manufacturing plants located in different parts of the country, and numbers among its products all of the manufactured forms of carbon. The most important of these are dry cells, motor and generator brushes, illuminating carbons, carbon specialties, and carbon and graphite electrodes.

The plant at Columbia, Tennessee, manufactures large carbon electrodes in order to meet a growing demand from the chemical and metallurgical industries of the South.

Maury County Ice Company.

The Gilbert MacWilliams Orr Collection

13

MAURY COUNTY REMEMBERED

Women at work in the Tennessee Knitting Mill.

Men working the looms at the Tennessee Knitting Mills.

MAURY COUNTY REMEMBERED

Wheeler Dam.

THIS PAGE
and
OPPOSITE
*Monsanto
Chemical
Company
drag lines.*

COLUMBIA
THE COUNTY SEAT

Columbia is a substantial city which has not allowed the progress it has made to steal away its cultural background, nor has it permitted the modern development it has enjoyed to cause its fine history to be forgot. Its citizens are courteous and hospitable in the busy pursuit of their economic existence; they are essentially and fundamentally American—the city is not, in any sense of the word, a "melting pot." But, lest a wrong impression be conveyed, it invites new citizens and new capital; it extends a welcome hand to those beyond its borders to come and visit or stay and dwell. Columbia is not selfish, cold, or snobbish.

Located 43 miles due south of Nashville, in the center of the bluegrass-limestone-phosphate section of Middle Tennessee, and in the area of the Tennessee Valley Authority . . . surrounded by agricultural lands as rich in soil fertility as any similar-sized region in America . . . possessed of resources, both natural and man-made, which tend to promote economic enjoyment . . . fortunate in commercial and industrial advantages . . . and having all social, religious, and educational benefits—Columbia offers opportunity!

COLUMBIA IS GROWING

During the past four years the population of Columbia has increased by more than 2,500 inhabitants who are now permanent residents of the city. Today there are approximately 12,000 people within its limits who call it "home." This healthy increase in population has been due largely to the expenditure, during this same period, of more than $5,000,000 for new private industrial expansion which has come about chiefly in the field of phosphate and chemical manufacturing. The government, through the agency of the Tennessee Valley Authority, has invested an amount in excess of $2,500,000 for phosphate holdings and for permanent improvement in the field of electrical power. TVA owns mineral rights in more than 1500 acres of phosphate-bearing lands. Another half-million dollars has been expended for business houses and for residences.

It is not unreasonable to believe Columbia will be a city of 20,000 inhabitants before another decade has passed.

COLUMBIA IS NOT AN UNUSUAL CITY

Like hundreds of other cities throughout the nation, Columbia has broad paved streets with trees along their borders which pass by substantial homes where a contented and industrious people dwell. The city has an excellent system of public schools which are second to none. Churches of all denominations afford places of worship for its citizens. Daily and weekly newspapers, libraries, social, and civic clubs fill a niche in the cultural life of the city.

Industrially, Columbia is developing rapidly and has enjoyed unusual prosperity throughout the last decade. This is largely attributable to the thrift of its people, to the natural resources which are to be found nearby, and to a rich agricultural section surrounding it.

POWER

The city is served with dependable and adequate electrical energy by the Columbia Power System, which gets its supply from four 44,000 volt "feeder" lines, chief of which is that of 110,000 from the TVA primary substation at Trans Crossing, and TEPCO furnishes its domestic and industrial

Mule Day–1940s. Marching band on West Seventh Street.

MAURY COUNTY REMEMBERED

ABOVE
Tobacco bound for market.

RIGHT
Traveling to Mule Day.

water supply. The largest primary substation of the Tennessee Valley Authority located away from the river is only four miles distant from Columbia. The field offices of this agency of the government are in the city.

TRANSPORTATION

Rail transportation is afforded Columbia by the Louisville & Nashville Railroad Company and by the Nashville, Chattanooga & St. Louis Railway. United States Highways serve the city North and South, while State Highways intersect here East and West. Excellent fields abound near the city

limits for airport facilities. Columbia is built along the banks of the Duck River which flows westward into the Tennessee.

MARKETING

Columbia is "the largest street mule market in the world." It is a center for the marketing of agricultural and dairy products which are produced in vast quantity round about it. The Columbia Livestock Market is a clearing house for this commodity which comes from the surrounding territory. In its own right, Columbia is a center of Maury County's livestock industry. Brown phosphate rock and phosphatic materials are mined "in Columbia's backyard" and pass through this city en route to the marts of the world.

RECREATION

An excellent nine-hole golf course is maintained at the Graymere Country Club, where also skeet shooting may be enjoyed by those who love the trap and gun. Tennis courts abound as does a park with diamond and gridiron. Boating is afforded devotees of this sport in the waters above the dam of the Tennessee Valley Authority within the city limits. The Princess and Lyric Theatres for pictures are spacious and commodious with every facility of modern equipment. The Tennessee Walking Horse abounds for those who love the saddle and the bridal path.

HISTORICAL

In Columbia is the ancestral home of James K. Polk, eleventh president of the United States. It is now a shrine with many of the original furnishings and has been restored as it was when this Tennessean lived there as a young lawyer before he scaled the heights to fame and greatness.

Here also is home of the late Edward Ward Carmack, United States Senator from Tennessee, and brilliant editor at the time of his death. A monument is erected within the city limits to the memory of Ed "Pop" Geers, immortal of the turf.

Princess Theatre—Bethel Hotel—West Seventh and N. Garden Street.

Columbia was the home of the former Columbia Institute, Episcopal School for Girls, founded in 1834 by Bishops James Otey and Leonidas Polk for the education of the young women of the South. And in other days the Columbia Athenaeum stood here as a place of higher learning for women from all parts of the country.

COLUMBIA MILITARY ACADEMY

The Columbia Military Academy is one of the oldest military academies in the South. It owes its foundation to the munificence of the United States Government. The school campus and buildings were transferred in 1903 by an Act of Congress to a self-perpetuating Board of Trustees for educational purposes exclusively. The Military Academy was organized in 1905 as a non-profit seeking institution, and has operated since that time under a Board of Directors for the sole purpose of developing young men in sound scholarship and forceful character.

The physical equipment of the school has been improved and enlarged through the years by the expenditure of many thousands of dollars. Recently two new dormitories have been added to accommodate an increased enrollment. The educational facilities of the school have kept pace with its physical growth. The faculty, enlarged from time to time, now consists of an unusual group of mature and experienced men.

The rating of the school, both in an academic and military sense, is the very highest. The school is fully accredited in all the educational associations of the United States and sends boys each year to the best colleges and universities throughout the land. The school has at its disposal, to fill existing vacancies, three appointments to the U.S. Military Academy and three nominations to the U.S. Naval Academy. These appointees and nominees are called Honor Graduates who, of course, rank high in scholarship.

Columbia Institute for Girls—West Seventh Street.

They are exempted from all mental examinations for entrance at West Point. The school has a fully organized R.O.T.C. unit.

The citizens of Columbia, in the constant expansion of the Academy, have played an important role. They have been loyal to the school and generous in every expansive

Dress parade, Columbia Military Academy, 1940s.

IN & AROUND COLUMBIA

Columbia experienced rapid industrial and economic growth during the first half of the twentieth century. Reasons for Columbia's growth include:

Wilson Dam with electrical generating equipment of 184,000 KW

Wheeler Dam with two 45,000 horsepower out-of-door type generating units

The largest primary substation of the TVA which is located off the river with 2 154,000 volt transmission lines coming into it and a third of similar voltage now under construction

The vast phosphate holdings of the Tennessee Valley Authority

Ferro-manganese is produced for the processing of steel

The largest and highest content of BPL phosphate deposits in Tennessee or any part of America, which deposits are of brown rock and are surface-mined

Hardwood which is readily transported to market by rail or highway

Coal and iron from mines less than 200 miles away

Electric furnaces producing elemental phosphorus

Soil that is fertile and productive,
rich in the mineral content of phosphate and lime;
and water that
abounds in these two elements

Broad level fields of large acreage
surrounded by tree-covered hills

Electric furnaces producing elemental phosphorus

The quick potential production of nitrates

Concrete arterial highways and large rail facilities
for transportation

White and colored labor in peaceful abundance

Taxing authorities who are reasonable
and possessed of a heart

Climatic conditions which afford practically an out-of-door life
for nine months of the year

Pastures of thick-sodded natural bluegrass
conducive to livestock raising

A territory that is far inland, but with quick
outlets in all directions

measure. The school belongs, in a true sense, to the City of Columbia. The Board of Directors and the Board of Trustees are all citizens of the community.

The grounds were purchased and buildings erected by the War Department of the United States Government as an arsenal. With 67 acres in the campus and ten stone and brick buildings in the physical layout of the school, together with equipment, this property is valued at more than one million dollars. Its location is at the western limits of the city of Columbia. Two important highways and the Cincinnati to New Orleans line of the Louisville and Nashville Railroad border its grounds. Many fine roads go through the campus, along which grow a varied species of trees. A natural amphitheatre for drill grounds and athletic field is centrally located on the grounds, and it is confidently expected that a stadium is to be built there at an early date by the government.

The school, for the last four consecutive years, has been rated by the War Department as an Honor School—the highest rank a military academy can gain.

Columbia is justly proud of Columbia Military Academy. Its cadet corps comes from 26 States and 4 Foreign Countries. It is an asset to this community.

TODAY

Rich in history, Columbia has its face turned to a new day. An appropriation of $340,000 has been made by the Congress for the erection of a P. O. and Federal Courthouse to be built of marble within the city. Ground will shortly be broken for this structure on a lot in the business district

West Seventh Street and the Maury County Courthouse.

which the government now owns. Work is being pushed on a program of expansion of the facilities of the TVA substation to meet a growing demand for cheaper power. It is confidently expected and believed from authentic sources of information that the sum of $750,000 will eventually be expended by the Authority here. Business houses are being built and renovated; new homes are everywhere in the course of construction within the city. Columbia's stores and shops are modern and smart. Its merchants are alert and progressive.

Columbia is definitely on the march to further development and to future progress.

Mule Day parade on West Seventh Street, 1940s.

THIS PAGE
*Mule Day
clean-up.*

OPPOSITE
*Preparing for
Mule Day on the
corner of South
Garden and West
Seventh Streets.*

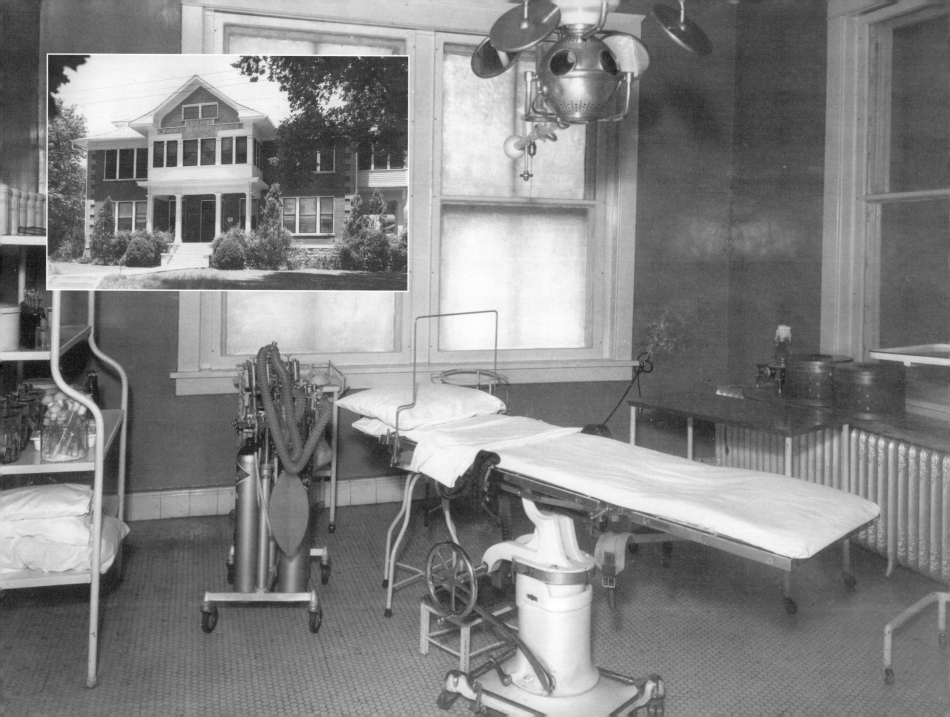

THIS PAGE
*Columbia Fire
Department.*

INSET
*Columbia Police
Department.*

OPPOSITE INSET
*King's Daughters
Hospital.*

OPPOSITE
*Operating Room,
King's Daughters
Hospital.*

INSET
St. Dominic's Catholic Church.

THIS PAGE
Old Catholic Church on High Street.

MAURY COUNTY REMEMBERED

TOP
St. Peter's Episcopal Church, West Seventh Street.

BOTTOM
First Baptist Church.

OPPOSITE
First Presbyterian Church, West Seventh Street.

The Gilbert MacWilliams Orr Collection

Hunters gather with fox hounds.

TOP
Awaiting the judge's decision.

BOTTOM LEFT
Calling in the hounds.

BOTTOM RIGHT
Tall tales around the fire.

HISTORIC HOMES

3

THE HOMES OF THE POLKS

At the mere mention of "The Polk Estate" in Maury County a host of dim memories arise like a veritable flood that brings in its wake the opulence of another day when peace and plenty reigned supreme until its was disturbed by the Civil War. And in this conflict-torn world of today this dignity and serenity of a past era comes like a benediction to bless the heart and mind that care for the more substantial things of the life in Middle Tennessee a century or more ago.

Col. William Polk lived at Raleigh, North Carolina. He was a wealthy banker and large land owner there. The elder Polks had promoted the Mecklenburg Declaration of Independence. They were a folk in whose veins the blood of liberty burned fiercely. They were soldiers all.

Tradition has it that Colonel Polk played the game of "Rattle and Snap" with the Governor of North Carolina and won a tract of 5,400 acres which lay in what is now Maury County. However, research reveals that this land was a grant to Colonel Polk for his services in the American Revolution.

Col. William Polk spent but little time in this new land where his vast acres lay. When he was here he stayed at "Will's Grove" near the present town of Spring Hill, but he divided his 5,400 acres among four of his sons who were a quartet from

James K. Polk Gardens in the spring time.

the 13 children by his second marriage. He had two children by his first marriage. One son, Hamilton, was born in what is now Rutherford County in 1810 and died in 1831. This son's death seemed to have weighed heavily upon the Polks, particularly the brothers who settled in Maury County.

In 1832 Lucius Polk built Hamilton Place, named for his deceased brother who died the year before. In 1836 Ashwood Hall was built by Leonidas Polk who was also one of the builders of St. John's Episcopal Church which was known as the "Chapel of the Polks." Rattle and Snap was built in 1845 by George Polk. Prior to the erection of these homes West Brook had been built by Rufus Polk who died in 1842 while his brothers were completing the house of worship nearby. Dr. William Polk, a son of Col. William Polk by his first marriage, built Buena Vista which stood where Columbia Military Academy is now located on the western edge of the city of Columbia.

All of these homes, with the exception of Buena Vista, were within a radius of one mile of each other and were located along the Mt. Pleasant Highway about six miles west of Columbia. West Brook was built to the south of the highway and was down a lane from St. John's Church. This home that Rufus built was burned after the Civil War. Ashwood Hall was located across the highway from the church and stood during the civil conflict but was burned in 1874. Buena Vista likewise passed by conflagration following the War between the States. Hamilton Place and Rattle and Snap are still standing today, the former being owned and occupied by direct descendants of the builder.

The acres of Colonel Polk and his sons covered many miles of what later proved to be the rich phosphate-bearing area of Maury County. These acres were situated within a belt of what is known as Maury silt loam, a soil as fertile as any to be found in America. The Gray farm, Ridley farm, Granberry farm, Yeatman farm, and the Armstrong farm have long been names to conjure with for beauty of landscape and fertility of soil. These farms were, and now are, tracts of from several hundred to more than a thousand acres each. They stretch out in panoramic splendor as one drives west from Columbia along the road that Old Hickory traveled when he was en route to New Orleans to do battle with the British in the War of 1812.

Hamilton Place

This home, built by Lucius Polk in 1832, is now owned by the grandson and the granddaughter of the builder. Here Mr. and Mrs. Trezevant P. Yeatman and Miss Jenny Yeatman now live where Lucius Polk brought his bride, the lovely Mary Eastin of Nashville, shortly after their marriage in the White House at

James K. Polk Home, 1940s.

Washington. Mary Eastin was a niece of Mrs. Emily Donelson, wife of President Andrew Jackson's secretary and mistress of the White House during a part of Old Hickory's administration.

Lucius Polk and his bride lived at "Will's Grove" for a time while Hamilton Place was being finished, a job that was thoroughly and meticulously done according to the wishes of this son of Colonel Polk. The brick for Hamilton Place were burned by the slaves and the timbers had been well seasoned after they were cut from the lands surrounding. Master workmen were brought from North Carolina to do the finishing construction work. How well these slaves and these imported workmen built is attested by the fact that today the house they constructed a century and a decade ago remains in perfect condition and is a picture of rare beauty.

Hamilton Place contains 13 rooms, seven of which are on the ground floor and six are on the second floor. This is exclusive of store rooms which are at the end of a wide porch that runs across the back of the house and the kitchen which is apart from the residence but is connected by a covered passageway.

Upon entering a hall in the front part of the house one comes to a longer hall that runs across the one at the entrance. At either end of this cross hall are beautiful spiral stairways leading to the second story. In this first hall today are sofas that were made especially for the spaces they now occupy and have occupied for more than a century.

The original furnishings of Hamilton Place are still in possession of the present owners and occupants. The halls have several large and handsome oil paintings, some of which are lifesize. Among the portraits are those of Col. William Polk, Lucius Polk, and Mary Eastin Polk. The period furniture is as lovely today as it was 100 years ago and the china and silverware are in exquisite and delicate patterns of a bygone age.

Hamilton Place.

Many famous persons have visited Hamilton Place, and until a few years ago the names of several of these were inscribed upon the walls of the upper porch. Andrew Jackson was a visitor there as was another president, James K. Polk. It is believed that Martin Van Buren also stopped at Hamilton Place, for there are today letters from his son to Mary Eastin preserved in this home.

Col. Harry Yeatman married the second daughter of Lucius Polk, Mary Brown, and they were the next owners of Hamilton Place. During the lifetime of this cultured and hospitable couple other notables visited their home. Among these were dignitaries of the church and writers of no mean note. Winston Churchill was an intimate friend of Colonel Yeatman. In his book, "Inside the Cup," he moulded, as it were, the character, Mr. Hodder, from the life of James Yeatman, a brother of Col. Harry Yeatman, and it was to him that he dedicated his book, *Richard Carvel*.

As was the way of building in that distant day the house was not completed without the garden. West of the mansion Lucius Polk had a beautiful garden laid out for his wife. It was planted with fragrant flowers, time-resisting boxwoods, rare shrubs, and lovely trees. The most conspicuous plantings were of magnolia trees which bordered the garden. They were shipped to Hamilton Place from Louisiana. Several of these trees remain today, one of which is thought to be the largest in the States—it measures nine feet in circumference. Its pure white blossoms in season still perfume the air at this ancient Polk estate west of Columbia.

Ashwood Hall

The second of the Maury County Polk homes, Ashwood Hall, was built under the direction of Leonidas Polk. It was started in 1833 when he brought his young and beautiful bride from North Carolina. He had been a cadet and was a graduate of West Point and later studied for the ministry. He was the

Ashwood Hall.

founder of the University of the South at Sewanee. He was the first Bishop of the Diocese of Louisiana, and was known as the "Fighting Bishop" of the Confederacy. In addition to his Tennessee lands he owned extensive acreage in Louisiana.

Leonidas Polk married Frances Devereaux. This couple lived at Hamilton Place while Ashwood Hall was being built. Mrs. Polk was a descendant of Johnathan Edwards of New England history and fame. She was a woman of strong character. Left 1,000 slaves under the terms of the will of her father, owner with her husband of vast lands in Tennessee and in Louisiana, she saw their fortunes wiped out by war, storm, and cholera. But she was as valiant in adversity as she was gracious in prosperity. She came back to Columbia in her later years and was a member of the faculty at the Columbia Institute for Girls, an institution that her husband had helped Bishop Otey to found.

Ashwood Hall was the most pretentious of all the Polk homes. It reached the zenith of its splendor under the ownership of another brother, Andrew Polk, who purchased it from Leonidas when the latter went to Louisiana in 1841. This home was then made into one of the handsomest in Tennessee and was the peer of any in the South.

The magnificent mansion was built in a grove of stately trees. There were one hundred acres in the lawn that ran down to the highway. Many of the trees there were indigenous to this section, but others were imported from foreign lands. Among these imported trees was a Ginkgo (maiden hair) which came from Japan. It has weathered the years and is now majestic in beauty and gigantic in size.

English Gardener

An English gardener was brought to Ashwood Hall to lay out and cultivate the gardens and to care for the lawn. The wife of Andrew Polk was the former Rebecca Van Leer of Nashville. The owners had their own greenhouses and many were the rare plants and flowers grown there to ornament the great house throughout the period that their home was the gathering place for the elite of their day.

For about a score of years preceding the Civil War life was gay at Ashwood Hall. The belles and the beaux gathered there as did dignitaries of more mature years. It was a center of activity and hospitality for the Confederate officers and a haven for those who wore the gray. It was here that the lovely and vivacious Antoinette Polk lived and reigned as a belle of her era.

This beautiful Antoinette Polk later became the Baroness de Charette. But before her marriage to this foreign nobleman and during the height of the Civil War she made a six-mile ride that has been famous in tradition for three quarters of a century. This has fired the spark of romance and has delighted the hearts of all who admire courage and horseflesh for all these generations past.

Miss Polk was visiting in the home of her uncle, Dr. William Polk, at Buena Vista. It was at that time that Wilder's mounted infantry, on a raid, rushed into Columbia. They had learned that certain Confederate officers were at Ashwood Hall. They determined to ride the six miles west of the small town of Columbia and capture these men of the enemy forces. But Antoinette Polk had other ideas which she put into execution in lightning fashion.

Warns Confederates

The Polks were among the first in Maury County to introduce the Thoroughbred horse. Antoinette slipped to the stables of her uncle, saddled a game bay mare, was up in a flash and started across the vast lawn toward the gate that opened on the Mt. Pleasant pike. A native Southern sympathizer saw her, sensed the situation, and flung wide the gate.

But the Federal cavalrymen were not to be caught napping. They started in pursuit of the young woman who carried the good blood of a long line of game and fighting ancestors. The bay mare carried the blood of "an hundred kings of the desert," and as she bent low upon the back of the speeding steed a purple plume was flowing backward from her riding hat as if to wave farewell to those who sought to overtake her. She left the Federals "as though they were tied to a fence," and she sped out the pike "like a winged angel on a beam of sunlight."

Needless to say, the Confederates were warned and made good their escape before Wilder's raiders reached the palatial home of this dashing young woman of the Old South.

But Andrew Polk, who had volunteered in the service of the Confederacy, was wounded in battle during the early part of the war. He then went abroad to live and died in Switzerland in 1875. The great house was closed after the Civil War and remained unoccupied until 1870, at which time Mrs. Sarah Polk Jones, a daughter of Lucius Polk, moved there and remained until Ashwood Hall was burned in 1874. So massive was the building and so solid the structure that it

St. John's Episcopal Church at Ashwood.

is said the ruins smoldered for two weeks after the flames had wrought their fury throughout the most pretentious of the Polk homes.

Historic Chapel of the Polks

Although Leonidas Polk was a military man and rose to the rank of Lieutenant General, and was killed at the battle of Pine Mountain, yet he was also a devoutly religious man.

After he had completed Ashwood Hall in 1836 he turned his attention to a place of worship in the vicinity where lived the Polks. To this end he donated six acres for the erection of a church. This structure he named St. John's Episcopal Church and patterned it after the style of architecture then prevalent in England which he had lately visited.

This brick church with ivy-covered tower stands today and is used once each year for worship in the Diocese of Tennessee. But it was 100 years ago, September 4, 1842, that the Chapel of the Polks was originally consecrated as a shrine, such as it has now become for Episcopalians throughout this section of the State.

The church is a simple but dignified structure. Its white walls and high ceiling, its plain pews and its floor of wide plank impress one, as do the simplicity and beauty of the Christian faith. The chancel rail around the altar is made of cherry wood, cut from a tree that once stood on the site. The marble baptismal font was donated by a daughter of Col. William Polk and a sister of Leonidas. During the Civil War the pews were pushed aside and the interior of the church was used as a temporary hospital for the wounded soldiers who were brought there for medical care and attention.

Bishop James Hervey Otey, first Episcopal Bishop of Tennessee, preached the sermon at St. John's on consecration day. A large gathering of prominent churchmen from Tennessee and other States gathered there on this occasion. And now, all four Bishops of Tennessee have stood in the pulpit where "The Good Bishop" preached a century ago.

In the churchyard many of the Polk descendants and others are buried. At one time four Confederate Generals were interred there, but their bodies have long since been removed to their respective States.

Each fourth Sunday in May a pilgrimage is made to St. John's at Ashwood. The Bishop of Tennessee preaches the morning sermon and is assisted in the rites of Holy Communion by the Rector of St. Peter's Episcopal Church at Columbia and the Priest in charge of the church of the Holy Cross at Mt. Pleasant. Other Episcopal clergy of Middle Tennessee are likewise there as are communicants from many cities throughout this section.

Following the morning sermon a pilgrimage is made to the tomb of Bishop Otey who is buried in the churchyard there. Flowers from the altar are placed on his grave, this being the concluding part of the service that is annually held at the Chapel of the Polks.

Rattle and Snap

The last of the homes of the Polks to be built in Maury County was Rattle and Snap which was erected by George

Polk in 1845. This magnificent mansion is on the south side of the Mt. Pleasant Highway half a mile to the west of St. John's Church and across the way from Hamilton Place which is on the north side of the road.

Tradition has it that the name of this home came about because two of the sons of Col. William Polk wanted this site that is somewhat elevated and which commands a vista of rare beauty looking through a grove of giant oak trees and across broad acres which lie to the north.

To determine which son should have this site the game of "Rattle and Snap" was resorted to as a means of decision. Whether this name originated because of this or because the venerable father of George Polk had played this game with the governor of North Carolina for the vast acres he owned in Maury County is probably one of the matters sometimes lost in antiquity.

At any rate, George Polk built Rattle and Snap for his bride who was Mary Hilliard of North Carolina. It is an imposing structure of twenty rooms and its white columns in front tower high to form an inspiring sight for those who go up the long driveway that leads from the pike to the big house on the hill. These columns are of stone and were shipped by water from Cincinnati to Nashville and thence drawn by ox cart to Ashwood.

Hides Silverware

It is said that during the Civil War the family sought a safe place in which to hide the silver "for the duration." A small son of the owners of Rattle and Snap was somehow

Rattle and Snap.

lifted to the top and was lowered by rope into one of the massive pillars where he placed this handsome silver. There it remained until the conflict was over.

The foundation of the house is said to be made of marble. The doors are massive and impressive. All the windows are made to reach the floor and they slide into the sidewalls. This was done in order that the occupants of the big house might have freer ventilation in the hot days of summer. The mantels are low and are made of Italian marble. They were carved in Italy and shipped here, each in one piece. The double parlors are on the left of the entrance hall and there are two great dining rooms that could be thrown together for a banquet hall on occasion of elaborate entertainment.

The stairway went to the second story of the house from a side hall and curved up to the third floor to what was called the attic, albeit the rooms of this "attic" are four in number and are massive in size. One may look upward from the first floor to the third floor, and he who looks cannot fail to be impressed with the rare beauty of these winding stairs.

Brick Kitchen

The kitchen was away from the big house and was made of brick. Servant quarters were over this kitchen. On the back porch were a series of bells, each of a different size and with a different tone. These were the "service buttons" of the house and the servants knew which room was calling by the sound of the bell. These bells, 10 in number, are there today silent with rust and devoid of the resounding ring that sent slaves scurrying almost a hundred years ago.

Three years after the Civil War Rattle and Snap was purchased by the late Joseph J. Granbery who reared a large family there. The new owner changed the name to Oakwood Hall and it remained in the possession of the Granberys for 53 years.

Now it is in other hands and is occupied by the overseer for the new owners and his family. But it is still known as "Rattle and Snap," and as one looks at this magnificent mansion today one cannot but somehow think of "the glory that was Greece."

And so the Polks lived and builded well. They wrought imposing and pretentious, but solid and enduring homes, where they typified most admirably the Old South that passed when war reared its hideous head. These homes have passed, all except Rattle and Snap that stands today in faded splendor—and Hamilton Place which lives in rare beauty and dignified serenity where the old and the new combine to carry on in a world that is again at war which envelops the globe.

THE HOMES OF THE PILLOWS

When Nashville was a mere village and Indians and bear roamed Davidson County a young man came on horseback to the opposite side of Cumberland River bearing a message to Gen. James Robertson. He halloaed across the stream where the ferry boat was tied up at the opposite bank. No one answered his call. He halloaed again. Then a young woman came to the boat, united it, pushed it off, jumped in, and rowed across the waters of the swollen river.

The young man was Gideon Pillow and the young woman was Anne Payne. It was love-at-first-sight with both of them. Three months later Anne Payne became the bride of Gideon Pillow at a wedding that was followed by an "infair," a three-day feast, where neighbors came to congratulate the bridegroom and to wish the couple happiness.

Gideon Pillow was a son of John Pillow, a grandson of Jasper Pillow, Jr., and a great grandson of Jasper Pillow, Sr., who emigrated from England to the Colony of Virginia in 1740. Jasper Pillow, Sr., had three sons—John, Jasper, and William, all of whom were Continental Soldiers in the America Revolution, and who continued in the service until the surrender at Yorktown.

John Pillow moved to the Cumberland River in 1784 and settled near Nashville. He had five sons—William, Gideon, John, Mordecai, and Abner, all of whom were engaged in Indian Wars. William was famous as a Colonel in the Indian Wars under Jackson, and at New Orleans. Gideon was conspicuous, along with William, in the battle of Nickajack.

Anne Payne was a daughter of Josiah Payne, Jr., and Mary Barnett Payne. Josiah Payne, Jr., was a son of Josiah Payne, Sr., and Anne Fleming Payne. Josiah Payne, Sr., was a son of George Payne and Mary Woodson Payne. George Payne, with his brothers, Sir William and Robert (afterward Bishop), came from Lancaster, England, to Virginia prior to 1700. The father of Anne Payne was a member of the Virginia House of Burgesses, an officer in the American Revolution, and a member of the Virginia Order of Cincinnati. Anne Payne was a first cousin of Dolly Payne Madison and of Lucy Payne who married George Washington Steptoe.

Gideon Pillow and his bride, Anne Payne Pillow, moved to Williamson County where they lived for a year or more. They then settled about four miles south of Columbia (what later was Columbia) soon after Maury County was formed in 1807. They built a log house near a big spring and near tall poplar trees on the south end of 5,000 acres of land which he purchased from the Nathaniel Greene grant.

This young soldier and hardy pioneer was a surveyor by profession. He was frequently away from home for days at a time. Once, while he was away, his young wife heard a noise in the pig lot one night. She knew what the trouble was, and, being without fear, she grabbed a shovelful of live coals from the wood fire, ran out of the house, and soon a bear was seen tearing through the canebrakes with his coat of fur burning fiercely.

The land they purchased was soon being cleared and planted. Their flocks and herds began to multiply. The whir of the wheel and the bang of the loom was steadily heard. Meat was cured, starch was pressed, soap was made. There were dairy products, poultry, and bees for honey. Cotton and wool for clothing and grain and livestock for food were being produced, and the Pillows were beginning to prosper.

The children of Gideon and Anne Payne Pillow were Gideon, Jr., Granville, Jerome, Cynthia, Narcissa, and Amanda. Each of these children grew to manhood and womanhood's estate and had children of their own. Each of

the three sons built a home on the lands which came to them by inheritance.

These three homes stand today, massive and imposing, and in such excellent state of preservation that one would not guess them to have been built a century ago. Two of these mansions are now owned by direct descendants of this pioneer couple, and one is occupied today by a great grandson and a great granddaughter.

The three daughters of Gideon and Anne Payne Pillow had issue of their own. These children have had other children until there are now in Middle Tennessee, and in other parts of the country, many prominent families who trace back to the young surveyor who was ferried across the Cumberland River by a belle who lived at Nashville when Gen. James Robertson was defending it and was guiding its destiny.

Cynthia Pillow first married John E. Saunders, scion of a prominent and wealthy Virginia family. They lived at "Melrose" which was, and still is, near Nashville. This magnificent estate became "the ideal home of the old South and the pride of all Tennesseans." The issue of this marriage were Narcissa Pillow Saunders, John Edward Saunders, and Cynthia Pillow Saunders.

After the death of Mr. Saunders his widow married Aaron V. Brown one month before his inauguration as governor of Tennessee. It was then that "Melrose," as the executive mansion, "had a career of unsurpassed distinction, the entertainments were many and lavish, and the home was visited by notables from every section."

Following his term as governor of Tennessee Aaron V. Brown became Postmaster General under President Buchanan. He died in 1860 and Mrs. Brown came back from Washington to "Melrose" where she lived with her children, one of whom was Granville Pillow Brown by her second marriage. She died at the age of 79 years and is buried at Mt. Olivet Cemetery, Nashville.

Narcissa Pillow married George W. Martin who amassed a considerable fortune in the mercantile business at Nashville. To this couple ten children were born while they lived at "Elmwood," a beautiful country estate of four hundred acres.

They later moved to Columbia and lived at "Mercer Hall," the former home of Bishop James H. Otey. After the death of Mr. Martin his widow continued to live at Columbia, although her plantations were in Arkansas. Her eldest daughter, Annie, married Col. Joseph Branch who was a partner of his mother-in-law in the operation of the cotton lands across the Tennessee River. During the Civil War they had 1,200 bales of cotton burned by the Confederates to keep it from falling into the hands of the Federals. Cotton, at the time, was selling for $1.50 per pound. Mrs. Martin died at the age of 72 years and is buried in the cemetery at St. John's Episcopal Church, Ashwood.

Amanda Pillow, third daughter of Gideon and Anne Payne Pillow, married Judge West E. Humphries of Nashville. They had three children and lived at "Vine Hill" which was not a great distance from "Melrose" and "Elmwood," the homes of her two sisters.

And, thus, we see the genealogy and the background, as it were, of this family and of the three brothers who built three homes in Maury County prior to the Civil War—in fact, a hundred years ago.

Clifton Place

Built in 1843 by Gideon J. Pillow, son of Gideon and Anne Payne Pillow, "Clifton Place" is the home today of William P. Ridley and his sister, Mary Ridley, great nephew and great niece of the builder.

Gideon J. Pillow was an eminent lawyer at Columbia prior to the Mexican War in which he served as a Major-General. After this conflict he returned to his home in Maury County and was a prosperous planter, owning lands there and in Arkansas. He served with distinction as a Brigadier-General throughout the Civil War and took part in many of the battles of the four-year struggle.

General Pillow married Mary Martin of Columbia. The issue of their marriage were Amanda, Gideon III, George, Narcissa, Lizzie, Annie, Sallie Polk, Gertrude, Alice, and Robert Martin.

"Clifton Place" is situated upon an eminence on the south side of the Columbia and Mt. Pleasant Highway. It is six miles west of Columbia. Here it has been a center of hospitality and social life for ninety and nine years. Today it

Mercer Hall.

contains much of the original furniture, silver, portrait paintings, and mirrors. It typifies the old South in its splendor and in its quiet dignity.

The mansion was constructed by slave labor, the brick having been burned on the place and the timbers having been cut from the lands surrounding it. The house has four rooms on each of the two floors. These rooms are twenty feet square. There are two large halls, one on the ground floor and one on the second floor. There is also a back stairway which leads up from the rear room on the right side of the entrance and goes into the upper hall.

The woodwork of the interior is of cherry wood, as is the grand stairway in the main entrance hall. This stairway goes up on the right and crosses over to enter the second floor on the left. From this stairway in October of this year lovely Sarah Ann Ridley, daughter of William P. Ridley and the late Eva Campbell James Ridley, tossed her bridal bouquet a few moments after her wedding vows to Charles Worthington Jewell of Franklin and Lexington, Kentucky. It was from this same stairway that another bride tossed her bridal bouquet half a century ago—this was Annie Gray Ridley, great niece of the builder, when she was married to William Parker Halliday of Memphis in 1892. Other brides of an earlier period, too, have ascended these stairs of cherry wood.

There are massive folding doors between the great rooms on both the right and left sides of the entrance hall. On the right and to the rear is the dining room which has been the scene of many banquets of state. On the left are the double

parlors which still have much of the original furniture to mark them with the beauty of another day.

The massive columns in front of the house are four in number. One is marred by the scar left from a hole that was cut into it. A cat belonging to one of General Pillow's children somehow fell into the top of this column. Slaves were summoned and a hole was cut to extricate the whining feline pet which was returned to its youthful owner.

In the rear of the great house are the brick kitchen, brick smokehouse, and brick carriage house, the latter being rather to the west down toward where the barns of the plantation were built. Further away down the hill are the "quarters" which contain the original cabins which housed the slaves in other days. To the east of the mansion is the brick office, a quaint but sturdy structure.

"Clifton Place," like many of the great homes of a century ago, had its garden which was planned in the same beauty and symmetry as the mansion. There was a central walkway bordered with boxwoods which have been well-clipped for a hundred years. The plot is a long panel that is divided into three sections—the first was planted to shrubs, the second to flowers, and the third to vegetables. It is thus today.

At the north-east end of the garden was a line of closely planted cedar trees that led to a wide terrace overlooking the fertile fields beyond. In other days this was the location of the greenhouse. Today it is the site of the home of William P. Ridley II (great, great nephew of General Pillow), and his wife, Eunice Holderness Ridley. Nearby is also the home Campbell Pillow Ridley, and his wife, Evelyn

Shapard Ridley, son and daughter-in-law of William P. Ridley, Sr.

Following the death of General Pillow "Clifton Place" passed to a son-in-law, H. Melville Williams, husband of Sallie Polk Pillow Williams. It later passed to James Webb Smith Ridley, father of the present owners and husband of Anne Lewis Pillow Ridley, she having been the eldest daughter of Jerome B. Pillow and Elvira Dale Pillow.

Under the ownership of Col. J. W. S. Ridley this farm became famous as a center of the mule industry of Maury County and the South. Thousands of young hybrids were fed there and driven afoot to the cotton sections of Mississippi and other southern states for sale.

Today there are 1,900 fertile acres surrounding "Clifton Place." This is one of the show farms of the South, known far and near for its rested state of fertility and high productivity such as only a master farmer like the present owner is capable of bringing about.

With its colorful century of history since General Pillow built this magnificent home should ever be entwined the thought of his brave mother, Anne Payne Pillow, who saved her son from the Indians when he was an infant. But for her fearlessness and her forthright courage there would have been no "Clifton Place" today or throughout the hundred years that now are past.

While her surveyor husband was away from home in 1807 a band of Chickasaw Indians came to her log home. Her one-year-old son was sleeping in his cradle. She fed the Indians and they left. One slipped back and stole the child.

The mother missed it, went through the woods as fast as she could go and soon overtook the chief of the band. She related her story. The Indians recovered her child and restored it to her arms. They then bound the guilty one and dragged him over the cane stubble where his bleeding body left its trail of blood through the wilderness.

Among Indians, one is considered base who eats his brother's salt and repays the kindness with an injury—and so, "Clifton Place" stands today.

Bethel Place

The second of the Homes of the Pillows was "Bethel Place" which was built by Jerome Bonaparte Pillow, a son of Gideon and Anne Payne Pillow. This mansion was finished in 1844 and was erected within a mile of "Clifton Place" which was built the year before.

Jerome Bonaparte Pillow was born in Maury County May 12, 1809 and died September 16, 1891. He married Elvira Dale of Columbia who was born on June 24, 1816 and died March 2, 1889. The issue of this marriage were Anne Lewis, Martha Woodson, Cynthia Saunders, Elvira, Fanny, Edward Dale, and Jerome Bonaparte, Jr.

Anne Lewis Pillow married James Webb Smith Ridley. She was the mother of William P. Ridley and Mary Ridley who now own nearby "Clifton Place," the home built by General Gideon J. Pillow, brother of Jerome Bonaparte Pillow.

Cynthia Saunders Pillow married William Decatur Bethel of Memphis. After the death of her parents this

couple lived at the home her father had built—hence, the name "Bethel Place."

This elegant mansion was constructed with slave labor, the same crew of workmen as built "Clifton Place." The brick for this house were dried on the land between the two homes. The old pit from which the clay was dug and the old kiln may be seen today along the line that separates the two farms.

In general lines of architecture this house is very like "Clifton Place," but there are sufficient variations as to make it individual in its own right. However, the foundations, brick walls, classic cornices, and Ionic columns are almost identical.

"Bethel Place" was set within a deep-sweeping lawn of bluegrass and ancient trees. Some of the tall pine trees are there today where they have stood as silent sentinels for almost one hundred years. The brick office of the plantation is in the side yard east of the mansion.

This home has ten rooms which include two on the wings. All rooms are large and with high ceilings. The woodwork is of cherry. The main stairway goes up from the large entrance hall in the front portion of the house. There are double rooms on the left of the entrance. These rooms have heavy folding doors between them. All doors of this, and of "Clifton Place," are massive and solid, and are done in beautiful design.

In that distant day bedrooms were frequently on the first floor. This is true of "Bethel Place." It was quite a task to have fires up stairs, huge open wood-burning fires were used and "back logs" were large and heavy to carry up to the second story.

The house has an upper balcony in front with a delicate woodwork baluster. In the rear of the mansion were two large and long porches, one up and one down. These ran the entire width of the house and had back stairways on either end of the lower porch leading to the one above.

Out back of the mansion, and at some distance away, was the brick kitchen, and another brick structure was probably used for servants' quarters. The brick stable was on the edge of the lawn and is there today, as are these other brick houses. In addition to these, and the office, there was a large brick smoke house where hung the meat from the plantation.

The garden at "Bethel Place" was somewhat similar to that at "Clifton Place." It contained boxwood borders and many rare shrubs and flowers that were popular a hundred years ago.

Jerome Bonaparte Pillow was a planter. He was successful as such. His acres were fertile and produced much grain and livestock, much cotton and wool. He was too old for service in the Civil War. He was past the meridian of life when the conflict began.

The land surrounding "Bethel Place" was the middle section of 5,000 acres owned by Gideon Pillow, Sr., father of Jerome Bonaparte Pillow. The lands of the three brothers, after their father's death, extended for almost three miles from the Campbellsville Pike on the south to the Mt. Pleasant Pike on the north.

This farm today is in a high state of cultivation. It is now owned by Sam Sweeney, Sr., who, with his son, Sam Sweeney, Jr., and wife, are considered farmers of the first order. In fact, Sam Sweeney, Jr., was named a Master Farmer of Tennessee a few years ago.

And so, "Bethel Place" and the acres around it blossom today as they did ninety and eight years ago when the mansion was finished by a son of Gideon and Anne Payne Pillow.

Pillow Place

At the extreme end of the Gideon Pillow tract of land in Maury County Granville A. Pillow, a son of Gideon and Anne Payne Pillow, built "Pillow Place" in 1845 and lived there until he marched away with the wearers of the grey as a Major in the Confederate Army of the South. He served throughout the civil conflict.

Granville Pillow married Olive Cheatham of Nashville. To this union three children were born. These were Susan, who married Hugh Martin; Granville, Jr., who married Mary Vinson; and William, who died unmarried.

The builder of "Pillow Place" chose the sight of his mansion where his father and mother had first settled when he came to Maury County in 1807. This was near the big spring and near a growth of giant poplar trees. It is said that pioneer settlers sought poplar trees which were an evidence of rich and fertile soil.

It was near the site of this home built by Granville Pillow that his mother tossed the coals of fire upon the back of the bear that was molesting her pigs one night. Here it was that a drunken Indian stole Gideon Pillow, Jr., when he was a year-old infant, but he was recovered by his brave and courageous mother.

The same slave workmen who built "Clifton Place" in 1843 and "Bethel Place" in 1844 constructed "Pillow Place" the following year as the third of the Pillow Homes in Maury County. The brick for the house came from the same kiln as those used in the other two homes.

This house was a delightful part of the social life of Middle Tennessee ninety and seven years ago and on up until the Civil War came to blight a way of life that never fully returned again. Many notables visited here in those ancient days and "Pillow Place" stood out as a splendid example of the embodiment of the old South.

This home is an exponent of the type of architecture that was prevalent at the time it was constructed. It has a dignified portico with Ionic columns of extreme heighth. Unlike the other two Pillow homes it had no upper balcony in front.

"Pillow Place" has eight rooms. Two on the lower floor are double rooms with folding doors between. One on the second floor is of the same type. The rooms are large and the ceilings are high. The woodwork is of cherry wood and the floors are of wide plank.

A distinguishing feature of "Pillow Place" is the spiral stairway that goes up from the front hall to the third story which is an attic. This attic has four rooms, but they are unused except for storage space. This lovely and different stairway winds from the bottom to the top of the mansion, and one may stand on the first floor and look to the roof with the staircase curling above like the coils of a corkscrew.

Back of the house was a brick kitchen. There was also a brick carriage house and a brick stable. Fine spans of horses were stabled at "Pillow Place" from an early day in the history of Maury County.

The garden was a lovely one. The boxwoods were huge. This garden and the box are gone in their live beauty today, but the house stands in the strength of its symmetry even as it has done for almost a hundred years.

Skipwith Place—Williamsport Pike. Current owner, H. L. Harlan family.

This home is owned today by Mrs. William Parker Halliday of Memphis, a daughter of J. W. S. Ridley and a great granddaughter of Gideon Pillow, Sr. It is occupied by Mr. and Mrs. Edward Thomas, he being in charge of the operation of the farm round about it.

This place is hallowed to all the long line of descendants of Gideon and Anne Payne Pillow who were among the last of a hardy race of pioneers who, by reason of and through their courage and hardships, helped to make possible the high state of civilization that is enjoyed by the generation of today.

Hallowed to their descendants? Yes, for the earthy remains of this surveyor and his wife have slept for more than a century in the garden at "Pillow Place," the scene of their triumphs in a land that was a wilderness when they were young.

STATELY MAURY HOME BUILT ON LAND GIVEN FOR SERVICES OF FAMED AMERICAN SOLDIER

Skipwith Place
Standing in stately grandeur that has been its own for almost a century and a half is Skipwith Place which is six and one-half miles northwest of Columbia on the Williamsport Pike.

It was named for its first owners, Peyton Skipwith and his wife who was Cornelia Greene, a daughter of Gen. Nathaniel Greene of Revolutionary fame.

This lovely home is located along the northern border of a 25,000 acre tract of land granted to Nathaniel Greene for his services in America's first war. The Skipwith acres were 1,100 in number and were given to the son-in-law of the famous old General.

The house, now in an excellent state of preservation, was built in 1800 and has been a center of culture and hospitality since Tennessee was young in the sisterhood of states. During the 142 years that Skipwith Place has stood it has been owned by only two families, that for which it is named and the Harlans, the latter being a family that has long been prominent in Maury County.

Peyton Skipwith was the oldest son in America of Sir Peyton Skipwith who built Prestwould in Mecklenburgh County, Virginia. When young Peyton and his wife came to Maury County, while this portion of Middle Tennessee was still a part of Williamson County, they brought with them many of the luxuries to which they had been accustomed. They had lived where beautiful gardens flourished. They brought rare plants and shrubs and laid out a magnificent garden at their new home in Tennessee. It was made in four squares and was filled with mimosa, lilac, and English box. There were many grape arbors, grapes for table use and grapes for making wine. The garden and yard were small—they only contained 23 acres.

The house had then and now has an ornate interior. The mantels were Sheraton and were handmade. The stair rail was slender and exquisite. The front walls of the house had wide boards and deep grooves. The clapboard on the wings was beaded on the bottom edges. In its early history a room on the second floor of the house was used to store coffins for the Skipwiths when they passed from labors to refreshment.

But in 1844, only 17 years after Columbia was incorporated, Skipwith Place passed into the hands of Maj. Ben Harlan who had only recently come to Tennessee from Kentucky. This young Kentuckian leased the farm in 1844 and five years later he purchased the land and house. The new owner changed the name of this famous old home to Oakwood Farm.

Major Harlan was a colorful character. He became a power in the political and civic life of his new county. His home became a center for purebred livestock. He loved blooded horses and game chickens. He was the soul of hospitality and while he was only a major, yet he was every inch of a "Kentucky Colonel." It is told that on hot summer days he kept a small Negro boy beneath the giant oak trees in his front yard with a cool bucket of water to quench the thirst of travelers along the road in front of his home.

This beautiful estate is known to Maury Countians who are now living as the Allen Harlan place. It was as such that further color and culture and hospitality were added to its already wide fame by Allen Harlan and his charming wife.

This son of Major Harlan was as fine a sportsman as ever witnessed a horse race or saw a cockfight. He inherited from his father a love of livestock. It was he who made three trips to Spain and purchased the best jackstock which that country had to offer. He brought the famous jack, Taxpayer, to Maury County and helped to build up the already well-established fame of this county as the center of the mule industry of the South.

Allen Harlan has now passed on but he held high the torch left him by his father who, during his lifetime, sent blooded livestock to Nashville each two weeks which then went by river to New Orleans. This son of Major Harlan held open house at his home where visitors came from Louisville, Cincinnati and other distant cities to see his horses and jacks—and incidentally, to witness some of the best cockfights that have ever been held in the South.

The home is now owned by Mrs. Harlan, widow of Allen Harlan. It stands today just as it did more than a century ago—stately, serene, hospitable. But during its day it has seen much of color and glamour, much of lives that were lived fully and were a benediction to all who came to Skipwith Place, which name it has borne since the late Allen Harlan brought his young bride to live on these broad acres which lie in the heart of Maury County's rich phosphate lands.

Reverend Frederic Augustus Thompson House and Garden

Here and there in the world of illustrious persons are sometimes found those who chose seclusion rather than yield to the beckoning finger of fame. Their genius is buried in the retreat of their preference rather than made to shine in the mart where the multitude clamors for the product of their handiwork or the creation of their brain.

Such was the life of Myra Thompson, daughter of the Rev. Frederic Augustus Thompson and Sarah Myra Holland Thompson, who spent the last four decades of her life at her girlhood home near Spring Hill. For reasons best known to herself she turned a deaf ear to the cry for her talent as an artist and lived alone with her beloved dog, Jacques, until her death just seven years ago.

The Myra Thompson Home near Spring Hill.

But the story of Myra Thompson begins a hundred years ago when her venerable and godly father built a home in Maury County three miles east of what later became the town of Spring Hill. This home was built by the compass so that it faced due west, and the fence around it was run by the compass, too. The two-story frame house was constructed of yellow poplar and it stands today in a remarkable state of preservation after weathering the storms since 1846, the year this Presbyterian divine married the daughter of James Holland and Winifred Sanford Holland.

Built Garden for Bride

This young minister built a garden for his bride, a garden that was famous for its symmetry of design, its many and rare flowers and shrubs, and one which yielded $4,800 to his daughter a few years before her death when she sold the boxwood to parties in New York. Plants from this famous garden were placed around the World War Memorial in Bronx Park, New York City.

The garden, planted by the builder of the ancient house, was 90 feet square with center circle and four surrounding ovals of boxwood. Walkways between the flower beds were originally six feet wide. Shrubs included althea, spirea, snowball crepe myrtle, Scotch broom, flowering almond, syringa, lilac, bridal wreath. There were pomegranate, japonica, spice honeysuckle, white jasmine, yellow woodbine, swamp dogwood, Arabian jasmine, and four-o'clock. Roses were Burr, Carolina Tea, Louis Philippe, Blanche Verbert, Maiden Blush, and Tilenburg.

Beds of flowering bulbs bordered three sides of the garden, the other side having been planted to mock orange trees. On two sides, beyond the bulb beds, were July apples and arbors of grapes.

The house that never changed throughout the almost 100 years of its occupancy by the Thompsons was built upon a portion of the estate that was purchased in 1809 by James Thompson, grandfather of the builder and great-grandfather of the artist who forsook fame and lived alone.

This ancient mansion is "L-shaped" and has eight large rooms, four on either side of two long, wide halls on each of the floors. It had a long back porch on the "L" that was enclosed with lattice work. The kitchen was built apart from the house. Here "Aunt Jane" presided and served her mistress long after she was freed from slavery at the end of the Civil War.

And it was to this house that letters came from Harriet Beecher Stowe, author of *Uncle Tom's Cabin*, which letters were to the old master of the mansion and were signed "Yours in Christian Love, H. Stowe." He was also a close friend of Henry Ward Beecher who wrote consoling him upon the loss of his slaves. These letters are preserved today in the marvelous and priceless scrap book of the late Mr. N. Douglas Martin, who lived at Hill Hurst Farm near Thompson Station until her death a few years ago.

Tribute by Niece

Mrs. Martin, a niece of the mistress of the old mansion, penned this about her aunt, the wife of the Rev. Frederic

Augustus Thompson, "She was a graduate of the Columbia Institute, a fine musician, most excellent housekeeper given to hospitality, the most wonderful entertainer of all who came under her roof. Her Christmas dinners, given to all of us, my father's family and all the extras we wished, were occasions never to be forgotten."

And it must occur to you, gentle reader, as it does to this writer, that to have sat at the table in this ancient house at Christmas with the godly Mr. Thompson at the head, flowers from the great garden nearby, and food prepared by "Aunt Jane," the old slave who wouldn't go free—well, certainly these must have been as Mrs. Martin said, "occasions never to be forgotten."

It was in the big yard surrounding this house that a cabin stood wherein one Harvey Watterson slept (and sometimes studied.) He was a student at the old Jackson College that was nearby. He won fame in his own right as a lawyer of no mean reputation and ability, but he was later the father of Henry Watterson, the late brilliant editor of the *Louisville Courier-Journal*. It was because of his illustrious son that he is known to the present generation, or perhaps, the generation just past—for who does not remember "Marse" Henry's famous editorial, "To Hell With the Hohenzollerns and the Hapsburgs" of a quarter century ago?

But back to the daughter of this couple who lived in the big house, "Miss Myra," whose portrait in early life shows her to have been a beautiful woman. She received the highest advantages of education and had the background of much culture and refinement. She studied art in New York

City and later went to France where she studied under some of the old masters. She did portrait painting and was reaching a high place in her chosen profession when the death of her parents changed the remainder of her life of 75 years.

Returns to Old Home
She came back to Maury County and went to her girlhood home. She lived there where her early years were spent and she lived alone. Occupying the back rooms of the house, she never allowed any change to be made from the way her mother and father had left the place when they departed this life.

Lace curtains hung at the windows, candles were half burned in pewter holders. Treasures in antique furniture were in every room—teaster beds of rosewood, handcarved tables with marble tops, paintings of an early period, priceless china and services of sterling silver. Literary gems of the world's choicest poetry and prose were in one massive book case and religious works were in another. The sermons of the Rev. Frederic Augustus Thompson, who studied to be a missionary to India but who preached at Spring Hill for 40 years, and "never took up a collection," were preserved intact in a handsome desk that was in the home.

"Miss Myra," during the four decades of her seclusion, sometimes painted for relaxation and recreation. She created in oil her father's garden, made sketches of her parents and of "Aunt Jane," and did such other painting as she cared to do with none to see but herself and her kinspeople and friends near the town of Spring Hill. But hers was a lone life because she preferred it that way, and it remained so until her death on July 4, 1935, when she had lived half a decade more than her allotted time of three score years and ten.

The old house still stands today. It is occupied by Raymond Parks. It was purchased by Miss Mamie Hatton, a daughter of General Hatton whose monument adorns the center of the square at Lebanon. The garden with the box-wood is gone, and so are the cabins that used to house the slaves before 1860—but the spirit of "Miss Myra" probably still worships at the shrine of her parents in the house that changed not for 40 years while she lived alone and dreamed of a past that never returned.

Wilson Place (The Barrow Place)

About 115 years ago a wealthy young planter came from Louisiana to Maury County two decades after it was incorporated from a southern portion of Williamson County. This rich newcomer was Robert Wilson who lost but little time in beginning the erection of a home for the young native girl he had wooed and won. She was Charlotte Armstrong, daughter of James Armstrong who was a Revolutionary soldier under Gen. Francis Marion who was known as "The Swamp Fox."

Young Robert Wilson chose a site for his home four miles south of the city of Columbia which had been incorporated in 1827, about the time of his advent into this section of Tennessee. He had purchased a large plantation which was located between the Campbellsville Pike and the old Jackson Highway, later the Mt. Pleasant Pike.

His vast acres joined those which Gen. Gideon J. Pillow had purchased from Gen. Nathaniel Green and where three stately homes that stand today were later built.

Wilson Place.

Raised Large Family

Robert Wilson was the father of a large family. Many of his descendants are living at Columbia today. His wife's father was among the first Presbyterians who came to Maury County and built the first Zion Presbyterian Church in 1806. James Armstrong was the progenitor of many who now rest where he is buried in this old Zion Cemetery. Many of his descendants are likewise living in Maury County today.

Wilson Place was built in 1830. The brick for the structure were pressed by the slaves on his plantation. The timber in the house were cut from his lands. How well the mansion was constructed is attested by the fact that it has stood for more than a century and today is in an excellent state of preservation.

The house is a fine example of early American architecture of that era. Its stately old square columns tower to the top of the structure. It has eight tall windows with 24 panes in each on the front side of the mansion. There was no upper balcony but a beautiful fan-shaped arch ornaments the portion of the front above the second floor door.

Inside are eight rooms that measure 20 feet wide and 22 feet long, four of these being on each of the two floors. There are two long and wide halls running the length of the house. The floors are made of white ash and the planks are wide and thick. The stairway is of the winding type and the woodwork is of cherry.

The mantels are things of rare beauty of the colonial type with stenciled decoration in antique lacquered gold. They are exquisite and lovely today.

Large Basement

Beneath the first floor is a basement with five rooms and the third story of the house is an attic that runs the length and width of the mansion. Beyond the house, but connected by a covered "dry" walk, is the kitchen that is made of brick. It has an open fireplace in it and a chimney for the stove. The servants' quarters also of brick, were back of the kitchen as was the huge smokehouse.

Robert Wilson and Charlotte Armstrong Wilson reared a large family at Wilson Place. Their daughter, Eliza, married a Doctor Fain, Martha married Vance Thompson, Leonora married a cousin, Flavel Wilson, John married Rebecca Fleming. The descendants of some of these, the Thompsons and the Flemings, now live in Maury County near the old Presbyterian Church at Zion where the builder of Wilson Place and his wife are both buried.

The youngest son, William, went to Texas at an early age. The house passed to him and from him it went to John D. Barrow who, with his family, lived there for more than half a century. The place is now in the possession of W. P. Ridley and Mrs. Andrew Dale with Mrs. Barrow retaining a life estate in the same.

Mr. Barrow was one of the largest livestock dealers in a long line of men who have made Maury County famous for its quality mules. It was he who sent the beautiful single hybrid to the St. Louis World's Fair which was declared the grand champion among all those which competed from every part of America. The handsome trophy won there is in the Barrow home today.

Mrs. Barrow, at 90 today, talks interestingly about the home where her beautiful daughters were born and reared. It is known to her, and to all who have lived at Columbia during the past half century, as the Barrow Place—and there it stands today looking as stately and as sturdy as it did when it was built by Robert Wilson 115 years ago.

Fairmount

Typical of the splendor of another day is Fairmount, one of the splendid landmarks in Maury County and a mansion that still stands three miles south of Columbia on the Mooresville Pike where it was built more than a century ago. Time has wrought changes round about it, but this fine old house is very like it was when John Smiser finished it in 1837.

The builder of Fairmount, this John Smiser who was a native of Hagerstown, Md., was married to Mary Evie Turney at Paris, Ky. He later came to what is now Maury County from Natchez, Miss., and was one of the first lawyers and an early

Fairmount.

sheriff in Williamson County. In 1814 he and his family came by river from Natchez and settled on the land where Fairmount now stands.

A vivid tale was left by the granddaughter of this Mary Evie Turney, telling how she was lost in the Shenandoah Valley in Virginia when a small girl. The posse of neighbors searched in vain a whole night through. Next morning at daybreak a hunter found the small child and a feast was held at the Turney home to celebrate the return of the lost member of this prominent Virginia family who were relatives of Peter R. Turney, onetime governor of Tennessee.

Owned Large Estate

Pioneer Smiser had a large estate. His first home was a two-story cedar lodge which was built in 1816. This was about a mile from the site of the present house and had a separate kitchen and slave cabins surrounding it. He began the erection of fairmount early in the 1830s and completed it 105 years ago.

Built of native timbers which were cut from the Smiser lands, and with brick which were made on the place by the slaves who lived there, this old house has stood against time and the elements, and today is in a splendid state of preservation. The lime for mortar was burned on the farm, and even the hair that went into this cement mortar was from the livestock which grazed on the broad acres there.

While most of the work on Fairmount was done by slaves it is well established by family tradition that master workmen who were imported for the job were paid the sum of

$9,999. This, it is said, did not include the hardware for the house, all of which was imported from England.

There were, and are, 12 rooms in the big house, and the third floor is a ballroom that extends the entire length of the mansion. There were two large halls running from front to back. These were covered with linoleum which was brought overland from Philadelphia. One piece of this linoleum was 19 feet wide and 30 feet long, and when taken up a few years ago it was still in excellent condition after it had been used for 100 years.

Died as Home Finished

But the builder of Fairmount did not live to enjoy the fruit of his labors. He died as the finishing touches were being made in 1837. His widow died a few years later and the big ballroom on the top floor of the house was silent and did not know the gaiety that was intended to dwell there.

Mr. Smiser and his wife are buried at Fairmount, as are other descendants who died in later years.

The house passed to his daughter, Ellen, who married James Gray Booker, scion of another wealthy family who lived on the adjoining estate. During the lifetime of the Bookers it is said that five horses stood on the lawn of Fairmount at one time. Four daughters and one son-in-law were stricken with yellow fever while visiting in New Orleans. They succumbed in the epidemic of 1852 and their bodies were returned by river to Nashville and were brought from there to Fairmount where they were buried.

A daughter, Mary Booker, married Britton Drake Clopton who was a native of Davidson County and came here from his home which was where Clover Bottom farm is now located on the Lebanon highway. They occupied Fairmount for many years and it is now sometimes known as the Clopton Place, a farm that originally extended from the Mooresville Pike eastwardly to the Pulaski Pike. It passed to the Bradley Frierson estate at the turn of the century. Later it was purchased by Bill Jones, of Birmingham, who did much to restore it to its former state. It was then sold to John H. Dinning, then to Doc Morris and 12 years ago it was purchased by Lex Watson, of Columbia, who now owns famous old Fairmount.

But the passing of years left a host of traditions and stories about this great house that is located atop a knoll that looks to the west. Many famous persons have been entertained there. Several generals of the Confederacy spent nights there. And Mrs. C. D. Anderson of Columbia, great-great-granddaughter of the founder, now has the china that was used to serve sumptuous suppers at Fairmount. She also has some of the original furniture that was in the John Smiser home.

And many are the tales that have fascinated descendants of this pioneer Maury Countian about "ghosts" at Fairmount. The slaves said that evil spirits haunted the big barns that were to the east of the great house. The massive square piano, sometimes in the still of the night, would be heard to play as if fingers were running the scales. And a beautiful lady in a fine carriage which was drawn by a span of pure white horses was said to have driven across the gravel roads that wound upward from the big pike to the big house on the hill—this was of nights when all was quiet on the estate that has been a part of Maury County for more than a century now gone by.

Thompson Place

Almost 200 years ago a strapping youngster first saw the light of day in Ireland. He was christened James by his parents who were Thompsons. His was a long and colorful life, most of which was lived in America to which country he emigrated in 1750. He was the progenitor of a long line of

*Captain Absolom Thompson Place,
near Spring Hill.*

his family, some of which descendants live at Spring Hill today.

When the town of Spring Hill was still a path for cattle and for hardy pioneers, James Thompson's grandson, one Capt. Absolom Thompson, came to Maury County from his native state Virginia. Captain Thompson was a builder. He erected a magnificent house which was to be the headquarters of General Hood during the skirmish at Spring Hill on November 29, the last year of the Civil War and on the night preceding the bloody battle of Franklin. With General Hood this night at the Thompson home were his adutant-general and Isham G. Harris.

Tradition has it that this James Thompson was kidnapped by a sea captain when he was a mere lad. He was brought to America and was apprenticed here. He vowed that when he reached manhood's estate he would go back to Ireland, find the sea captain and give him a sound threshing.

Threshes Sea Captain

Further tradition is that he did reach the peak of his physical prowess, he did return to Ireland, he did find this sea captain, he did give him a threshing, and when he had beaten the captain to a degree that satisfied him he caught the next boat and came back to America, a land he had learned to love.

The children of James Thompson were Andrew, Matthew, James, and John. The latter was the father of Capt. Absolom Thompson who was born in Virginia in 1800 and who came to the wilderness of Maury County about 25 years later. Captain Thompson, like his grandfather, was a hardy fellow in his own right. He was three times married. His first wife was Elizabeth Campbell, his second was Mary Langford, and his third was Mary Brown Sanford.

To the union of his first marriage was born the Rev. Frederic A. Thompson who was the father of Myra Thompson the artist, she who lived alone for 40 years in the house her father built across the road from the one her grandfather constructed about 1835.

His second wife, Mary Langford, was a daughter of Col. J. T. Langford, a member of the Congress. It was soon after his marriage to Miss Langford that Captain Absolom Thompson came to Maury County.

When he reached the land that had been a part of Williamson before he reached it, Captain Absolom looked about for a site for his home. He was a large landowner and had 150 slaves. He was a staunch member of the Presbyterian faith and was strong in his belief of the doctrines of this church.

Slave Labor Used

He and his slaves erected a mansion that stands today about three miles east of Spring Hill. It stands among the giant trees that were twigs when he planted them. The ancient boxwoods border the walk to his great house that bespeaks strength and character. It is well preserved and is an imposing structure of grey brick with square towering columns that reach the top as they go past an upper balcony that has a delicate iron grill around it. The great windows

MAURY COUNTY REMEMBERED

have four blinds and the glass arch over the massive front door is a thing of rare beauty.

This Thompson Place has 14 rooms which are 21 feet square. It has a big basement with four rooms. The lower floor has double parlors that could be thrown together by the use of beautiful folding doors. The front hall is 42 feet long and the floors are made of white ash in planks five inches wide.

The master of the house and his slaves did the actual construction work on the house, but workmen were imported to finish the interior whose woodwork is of cherry. The stairway from the hall starts on one side, crosses over and enters the second floor from the opposite side. It is a handsome work, this stairway. There was also a back stairway that was of lesser grandeur, but of substantial structure as was all else in this house.

Captain Thompson's second wife died, and to his third marriage, that with Mary Brown Sanford, was born a son, James Turner Sanford Thompson who was to become a doctor and who was to serve as a surgeon under Gen. Albert Sidney Johnston and as a scout under Gen. Nathan Bedford Forrest during the Civil War. This son was five times captured by the Federals. At great risk of life he escaped each time he was captured "preferring death to imprisonment."

Hood Slept There

This house passed to Dr. James Turner Sanford Thompson, but almost a score of years before that date General Hood had spent the night there. He slept in one of the rosewood canopy beds that were a part of the furnishings in each of the bedrooms at Thompson Place. This bed and some of the other handsome furniture is now owned by a granddaughter of Captain Thompson, Mrs. Myra McKissack of Spring Hill.

The General must have slept well and quite soundly, for the Federals passed on during the night and set up the death-trap for his troops at Franklin next day.

More of rumor than of Thompson tradition has it that the General did imbibe quite freely of spiritous liquors on this night of November 29, 1864, but his condition as to being drunk or sober or merely slightly intoxicated is a moot question that this writer dares not answer here.

But, if whisky was served the General it must have been brought in by his own waggoners and not by the slaves of Captain Absolom who was a devout churchman and one of the first elders of the Presbyterian Church at Spring Hill. His obituary, following his death on February 17, 1881, says he contributed largely to the church, was a regular attendant at the services and was never absent from prayer meetings. He was a promoter of the old Jackson College that was once near his home, and withal the Captain was a public-spirited citizen of his community.

After the death of the builder of this stately old mansion it passed to his son, Dr. James Turner Sanford Thompson who married Mary Leonora Cheairs. To this union eight children were born. These included Mayes, St. Clair, Susie Pointer, and Hattie Cheairs, the last named having married N. Douglas Martin, but all four of whom are now deceased. His children who are living today are Mrs. Myra Thompson McKissack and

Leo Thompson of Spring Hill, Miss Minnie Thompson of Washington, D.C., and Fred Thompson of Hargill, Texas.

The distinguished father of these children died unexpectedly in the prime of life and his widow remained at the old home where she reared and educated their children. At her death in 1910 the ancient house passed out of the possession of the Thompson family where it had remained for almost a century.

Thompson Place, unoccupied today, but sturdy, strong, stable, quiet, dignified, and a monument to pioneer Tennessee construction, is now owned by Mr. and Mrs. Ronald Voss of Nashville.

Cheairs Place

A Huguenot was born in the southern part of France early in the 18th Century. A house stands today in the northern part of Maury County in the 20th Century. The connection is that this is the house that the great-grandson of the doughty old Frenchman built.

Nathaniel Cheairs, Huguenot, came to America when he was a young man. He settled on the eastern shore of Maryland. The descendants of his son, Benjamin, settled in Florida and spelled their name "Chaires." Another son, Nathaniel II, settled in Queens County, Maryland, retaining the original spelling of the family name, and after the American Revolution moved to Richmond County, North Carolina.

Nathaniel II was the father of six children. These were Elijah who moved to the West when it was "wild and wooly" and, with his son, fought in the Mexican War, for which services he received a large grant of land. Benjamin settled in West Tennessee. Sophie was an only daughter. Vachel and Thomas remained in North Carolina where the latter became the president of a medical college in that state.

The Nathaniel Cheairs Place, near Spring Hill.

Nathaniel III, the other son of Nathaniel II, was born January 4, 1764. He married Sarah Rush, 14 years his junior, July 4, 1795, she being the daughter of William and Abigail Ferrell Rush. This couple moved to Maury County, Tennessee, in 1810, just three years after their new home had been created from a portion of Williamson County.

Selects Home Site

Nathaniel Cheairs IV was a son of Nathaniel Cheairs III and a great grandson of the old Nathaniel who had come from France. He married Susan McKissack and was a prosperous planter for a score of years preceding the Civil War. He selected the site for a home one mile south of Spring Hill on the Columbia Highway, called the "Pike of Battles" by the late John Trotwood Moore.

This fourth son of the name in the Cheairs family was a meticulous builder. He started his house in 1851 while he was living in a brick structure that was later the servant quarters for the mansion. He preferred to be near the place where his new home was being built so that he could better supervise the construction. The walls started up three times and three times they were pulled down because they didn't quite suit the master. Slave labor was plentiful on this land which was said to have been a portion of a grant from President Madison in 1810.

The mansion was completed in 1855 and became a center of social life in the Spring Hill community. There were four large rooms on the lower floor and the same number on the second floor. On the right of the entrance were the double parlors while the rooms on the left were separated by a hallway that came in from the side entrance. There was a beautiful winding stairway that went to the third story which was an attic. The woodwork and interior finishings were ornate but were in keeping with the dignity of the mansion. The furnishings were likewise of the style and quality befitting the period and the great house which held them.

Blythe Place.

But the shadows of war were lengthening and in 1861 the master of the mansion rode off as a major in the Army of the Confederacy and was made a prisoner of war in 1862 when Fort Donelson fell.

Two years later the war came to the very doors of the home Major Cheairs had built and had left when he marched off as a wearer of the Grey. On the night of November 29, 1864, the armies of Hood and Schofield collided about Spring Hill and the Confederates were bivouacked on the Cheairs farm. Many of the troops were in the spacious bluegrass lawn of 100 acres and slept beneath the giant beech trees there.

During this night a spirited skirmish took place in front of this house along the dusty pike that led south to Columbia and north to Spring Hill and Franklin. Hood slept at his headquarters at the Capt. Absolom Thompson home which was three miles east of the Cheairs place. He must have slept exceedingly well for history has it that couriers from the officers under him could get no answer from the general, and history has it further that the Federals went on to Franklin and set up the slaughter house for the Confederates next day.

Generals Dine at Home

But before death came to five of the generals who died at Franklin they had been guests of Mrs. Cheairs at breakfast that morning. These officers, and as many more as could eat there, were fed by the mistress of the mansion. But this quintet of high-ranking officers of the Confederacy, Generals Cleburne, Adams, Gist, Granbury, and Strahl, took their last meal here. That night they lay dead on the porch of the old McGavock home at Franklin. All of them were buried temporarily at St. John's Church at Ashwood in Maury County, to be disinterred later and removed to their respective States.

The great house passed to William M. Cheairs, a son of Maj. Nathaniel Cheairs, the builder. It remained a center of hospitality under the ownership of William Cheairs until 1920 when it was sold to John Whitfield, iron and coal magnate of Birmingham, Ala., who is said to have been attracted by the beauty of the place in passing and that this subsequently led to his purchase.

Mr. and Mrs. Whitfield made extensive improvement by giving a more modern touch to the interior of the old mansion. The walls were repapered and the woodwork was redone. The stairway was divided with the bottom step in the center of the great hall in front. The two rooms on the left were thrown together and modern fixtures were installed throughout the house.

The new owners occupied the old Cheairs place only a few years and sold it to Paul M. Davis and P. D. Houston of Nashville. The house is now unoccupied but it stands stalwart and strong today among the giant beech trees just as it did when it was built more than four score years ago.

Manor Hall.

Dr. George
Williamson
Camp.

*Central Christian
Church.*

Samuel Mayes Home.

Ferguson Hall.

Warfield Place.

FARM SCENES

4

Some early memories of a boy who lived in the city upon visiting his grandfather's farm way down in the country:

The prick to bare feet when going through a stubble field . . . doves coming in to a watering place late in the afternoon . . . red June apples; also horse apples and "rusty coats" . . . trips at dawn to the river to find a willow bush shaking, and taking catfish off a trot line . . . following the binder around a wheat field, stick in hand, watching for young rabbits . . . hunting eggs under the barn . . . cucumber pickle put up in ten-gallon crocks of brine that would "float an egg" . . . winter cabbage with straw over them under a low "shed" along the back of the garden . . . encountering hissing geese upon entering the barn lot . . . turning the big jar of milk in front of the wood fire . . . baths in a zinc tub when we couldn't go to the creek . . . cooking dinner for the thrasher hands at wheat harvest . . . riding the end of the coupling pole when the log wagon went to the woods . . . bluebirds nesting in fence posts . . . slick rocks in the spring branch . . . preserves and jellies in fruit jars and glasses down in the cellar . . . bringing in stove wood from the nearby woodpile . . . cracking scalybarks with a flat iron on the wide arm of an old rocking chair . . . trying to get guinea eggs out of a nest with a spoon . . . waiting to lick the dasher from the ice cream

ABOVE
Summer time on the farm.

LEFT
Baby chicks in the spring.

freezer . . . turning the grindstone to sharpen the axe . . . trying to hit bats with a fishing pole as they came out from the eaves of the house in late afternoon near sundown . . . woodpecker holes in dead sycamore trees . . . taking baby chickens off the nest (and being afraid of the hen!) . . . being waterboy for the men of the thrasher crew . . . a piece of pie or custard from the tin front perforated safe in the corner of the dining room . . . boxes of stick candy from the country store thinking the man who "broke the colt" was a hero . . . blowing up hog bladders with the joint of a cane and saving them to dry for Christmas when we jumped on them and made

them pop . . . ring of the anvil at the blacksmiths' shop . . . water moccasins under flat rocks in the creek . . . jars of milk in the spring house.

Beating tin pans to swarm bees . . . licking the honey from "tulips" off a poplar tree . . . sharpening a pocket knife on the whetstone at the blacksmiths tool counter . . . hunting certain kinds of plug tobacco tags and swapping them for stick candy and crackers at the store . . . drawing water from the well near the back door . . . watching "wiggle-tails" in the rain barrel . . . seeing Grandpa cultivate the garden with a "push plow" and thinking he was strong as a horse . . .

hanging around the cider mill . . . fighting off the little gnats that gathered and feeding the pressed pulp to the hogs . . . cleaning the lamp chimney with paper . . . wasp nests in the "outhouse" . . . a nap after dinner on a quilt under a shade tree with a straight chair turned down for a headrest . . . "silver sides" and "top waters" in the spring branch . . . sliding down the cellar door . . . listening to mules bite the corn off the ear . . . the sting of the cow's tail on the face at milking time . . . turtles sunning themselves on a log in the pond . . . taking "a turn of corn" to the mill on horseback . . . helping to turn the sausage grinder . . . a barrel of sugar in the closet under the stair steps . . . being "almost grown" when you could hitch the horse to the buggy . . . peaches and apples drying in the sun on top of the smokehouse . . . seining for minnows in the creek . . . horses hitched under the trees around the church and dinner on the grounds after the morning service . . . hams hung up with hickory bark . . . grinding Arbuckle coffee in the coffee mill . . . running errands for grandma (which were many) . . . shooing the flies off the table with a peach-tree limb . . . watching the hogs wallow in the mud . . . fans made from a turkey wing . . . stopping up the chicken coops at night . . . thinking it would be easy to hoe a row of corn . . . playing in the potato house . . . martins flying around gourds hung on a high pole . . . wondering why the rooster cackled when the hen laid the egg . . . a climbing rose in a frame at the south chimney . . . knowing that cold weather was near when horses romped and trotted with high head across the pasture . . . pumping the bellows in grandpa's shop . . . trying to chew beeswax . . . visiting the

Garfield Webster with country hams.

tenants on the farm (and playing with their children) . . . riding the wagon from the gravel bar when the men were working the road . . . hanging around the sorghum mill . . . being scared when the preacher came for dinner on sunday . . . pouring wood ashes in the ashhopper . . . quilt frames suspended from the ceiling . . . watching cattle lick salt . . .

"A mess of fish."

seeing "Aunt Louise" the cook, smoke her clay pipe . . . family prayers by Grandpa every night . . . storm curtains on the buggy . . . barbecued kid on the Fourth of July . . . pears on a tree they said was a hundred years old . . . sliding down the straw stack . . . playing in the tool shed . . . looking at pictures through the stereoscope; and a peep, every once in a while, at the family album in the parlor . . . rings around fruit trees made by sapsuckers . . . listening at night to frogs in the swampy ground and trying in vain to find them next day . . . cracklin bread and chitlings . . . breaking the old hen from setting by ducking her in the branch . . . biting green persimmons . . . turning the corn sheller at the barn . . . catching lizards with a looped piece of grass . . . hunting for pearls in mussel shells . . . smoke in your eyes from the wash kettle . . . tooth brushes from althea bushes . . . a skinned cedar tree used for a rack to hold the milk buckets and other vessels to sun . . . horsehair seats and an old organ in the heavy carpeted parlor . . . abdominal misery from eating too many green apples . . . homemade lye soap from meat skins . . . the first phonograph with cylindrical records and a tin horn . . . dirt dauber nests on the walls of the saddle house . . . trying out a new buggy whip to see how limber it was . . . the old wooden clock on the mantle piece with its metallic striking . . . ransacking the tray of Grandma's trunk . . . all the fried ham, red gravy, and scrambled eggs you wanted for breakfast . . . a trip to the cotton gin . . . carving initials on the old beech tree . . . cutting buckeye switches and throwing the buckeyes while still on the switch . . . thinking the village blacksmith was the leading citizen of the community . . .

MAURY COUNTY REMEMBERED

ABOVE and RIGHT
Harvested tobacco bound for market.

picking out black walnuts with a horseshoe nail . . . wondering why the cow "went dry" . . . eating blackberries off the bush . . . watching king fishers and "shike-pokes" fly up the creek . . . the glass on a shelf for Grandpa's teeth . . . new shoes of the older ones that "squeeked" when they walked . . . Grandma's home remedies when we had the "stommick ache" . . . waiting for plums to turn red in the plum thicket . . . the cruelty of having to eat "at the second table" when company came . . . holloaing down the rain barrel . . . listening to the owls "screech" at night . . . the beauty of a new saddle . . . popcorn balls made with sorghum molasses . . . pills in a pillbox . . . taffy candy pulled in the kitchen and cut on an oilcloth-covered table . . . Dutch, the bay buggy horse,

and Nellie, the grey saddle mare . . . the old covered bridge . . . ambrosia at Christmas, and strings of popcorn for Christmas tree decoration . . . sparks from the back log . . . winter evenings before an open fire.

TOBACCO

Interest was mounting today in the formal opening of the burley season at Columbia Wednesday. Farmers and growers of this section have placed more than 200,000 pounds of the golden leaf on the floor of the tobacco warehouse here.

During the past weekend crops from Maury County were brought to Columbia in car, wagon, and truck. A double line was on two streets here Friday and Saturday. They brought approximately 90,000 pounds of burley per day. About 25,000 had been placed in the flat baskets on the floor here this morning.

Maury County Tobacco Warehouse poster, 1940s.

So great was the rush of the "lineup" that many growers became tired with awaiting their turn and carried their crops to Mt. Pleasant. There they had the choice of placing the leaf on the floor of Maury County Warehouse No. 1 or on the floor of the Bluegrass Warehouse. These two houses, together with the one at Columbia, are operated by the Maury County Tobacco Warehouse Company. The combined floor space of the trio of houses is in excess of 220,000 square feet.

Just what the market price will be Wednesday when the 1941 season opens is a matter that veterans predict upon but lightly. They say the quality of the leaf this year is excellent. The pounds are lighter than last year but they believe loss in pounds will be more than offset by the gain in quality.

The big thing this year that is making growers of burley believe in Santa Claus and to venture the assertion that Christmas will be a merry one is a new setup, as it were, in the marketing of their crops.

USDA at Washington announced Friday that the Commodity Credit Corporation will make available a loan and purchase program for the crop that is now being readied for the current market. This, growers say, will give the assurance of a full price for their weed.

When the burley is graded by government experts a price will be placed upon it. If this tobacco does not bring that price on the open market under the "cheery chant" of the auctioneer it may be placed in government warehouse and the local company will pay the grower the price fixed by the inspector.

If this crop sells for a higher price later in the season, then the grower will receive the advantage of the advance; if it sells for less, then the CCC will absorb the loss.

With the parity price of 23 cents on burley there are many here today who are saying that the average Wednesday will hover around $30 per hundredweight. If the price breaks and holds around this mark—well, Santa Claus will have a clear track to the stockings of many guys and girls here this Christmas.

LIVESTOCK

Cattle leads in the livestock industry, with sheep and hogs being second and third respectively in number and in value by dollars. Thick sodded pastures of bluegrass are supplemented by winter cover crops to make year-round grazing possible without the trouble and expense of grain feeding.

This county is famous for its Jersies, both milk cows and herd bulls. The Jersey of this section produces milk that is high in butter fat content. More than 200,000 pounds of raw milk is produced here each 24 hours. This supply finds a ready market at creameries where it is treated and shipped to other cities, or is made into cheese at local plants.

An artificial breeding association for dairy cattle, the only one of its kind south of the Mason-Dixon line, has been established with headquarters in Maury County—it now has a membership of 150 dairymen and 1500 cows listed from artificial insemination. Its ultimate purpose is for the betterment of the Jersey breed and for the increase of butter for content in milk production.

There Is No Perfection in Dairy Cattle

That there is no perfection in dairy cattle, none who thinks twice will deny; but this is likewise true with those who breed other types of livestock. The horseman strives toward perfection, so does the herdsman and the shepherd and the porcine fancier. But man is not perfect.

Yet the strides that have been made toward improving the Guernsey breed of dairy cattle is a monument the thought and effort of owners of these fawn and white cows have built throughout almost ten centuries, that they have fancied these beautiful animals which give an abundance of rich and golden milk.

Karl Musser says, "In America, more than any other country in the world, we desire perfection. Individually, and in groups, in every line of endeavor, progress is made. The breeding of purebreed dairy cattle is no exception. Thousands of breeders have found fascination and profit in breeding toward perfection. While great strides have been made, there exists no finished breed. Those able to fix desirable characteristics of production, as well as beauty of form, reap a harvest recogniton together with a financial reward."

It is a business, so why not go at it in a business manner? Why not work for and find that satisfaction which comes to one from a degree of excellence which is above another who stirves in the same field to produce the best? There is a joy in competition. That is why men enter their individuals in the show arenas of the livestock world.

To breed better dairy cattle and better horses, sheep, and hogs is not only to produce champions and to feel the sweet taste of winning in keen competition, but it is to bring into the world individuals which serve man in a better and larger way. A purebred animal of any livestock type is not only a more beautiful animal but is one which renders a greater degree of service in the field that helps to feed, clothe, and recreate the nation.

A herd of Jerseys on the George Campbell farm in Spring Hill.

Who Produces Champions?

It is not always the big fellow who brings into being the great of any breed of any type of livestock. Often the small farmer excels all others in competition.

In 1940 at the National Dairy Show it was Smuggler Farm Reward's Lass which was grand champion Guernsey cow. She was bred by a northern Vermont farmer, Frank L. McCarthy, who owned a small herd. The year before that at San Francisco at the National Dairy Show on Treasure Island the champion female Guernsey came from the farm of D. R. Hughes in the State of Washington. This could go on at great length in the dairy world.

Where did the champion walking horse of the world come from in the two years above mentioned, 1939 and 1940 (and again in 1941), at the Tennessee Walking Horse National Celebration at Shelbyville? Both of them came from the "hills and hollows," and small breeders bred them.

Other Guernsey Champions

Claremont May Rose is one of the great foundation cows of the Guernsey breed. She was bred by a small farmer on the Island of Guernsey, the beauty spot in the English Channel. Her rich inheritance for type and production continues today in hundreds of thousands of purebred Guernseys in America.

Mixer Faithful, another great foundation Guernsey cow, died recently at the advanced age of 22 years. Her 10 sons and six daughters have more than 4,000 progeny in the Herd Register of the American Guernsey Cattle Club.

This great cow was sold at public auction at 7 years of age for the sum of $12,700 which seemed a fabulous amount, but her offspring had returned her owner many times the amount of the original purchase when she died.

Not all farmers and breeders, to be sure, can afford to purchase expensive stock, but they can watch what they are buying and get the blood of the champions and with proper care and judicious mating they can improve their herds. They can purchase purebred sires and build their herds to a higher state of perfection. They can purchase heifers which have the "rich inheritance" and with proper care and proper feeding, and by mating with a purebred sire, they can produce individuals which may not be champions—but they'll be better for type and production than those which come from haphazard methods in livestock breeding.

Why Not Herefords on Mid-State Farms?

Last week we were speaking of the Hereford's "aptitude to fatten" as learned from our recent talk with R. J. Kinzer, secretary for the past thirty years of the American Hereford Association. He was telling us how the use of Hereford bulls on herds on the range had brought about a 40 percent increase in weight of the steers and he said this was produced in less than one-half the time formerly required to tip the scales at around 700 pounds at less than two years old. This, he said, applied on farms as on the range.

Not only is the Hereford possessed of an ability to turn grass into profit, but the cow, steer and bull are found to be "rustlers." "When the feed gets short in his immediate vicinity the

Kana Domino, a champion bull.

Hereford does not come up to the barn and wait to be fed—he goes out and rustles up something to eat," Kinzer said. "And when he finds this substance he puts it into his body where it will in turn render the owner a profit. This natural aptitude to fatten readily and quickly is indicative of the economy with which the feed provided is converted into beef that brings a pretty good price on the market," he added.

Adaptability

When the beginner in beef cattle raising considers the various breeds from which to make his selection he should choose the one which is adapted to the environment existing on his particular farm. According to Kinzer, the Hereford is the most adaptable of all the breeds.

The success with which the fame of the Herefords has spread all over the world is proof indeed of their adaptability to various conditions, it was pointed out by Kinzer. This is, above all, he said, the outstanding characteristic of the breed and is largely responsible for their popularity and general distribution.

He said they were produced successfully from sea level under tropical conditions to the timberline in mountain ranges, and from semi-desert areas to the fertile corn belt states. "Why not more on farms here in beautiful Middle Tennessee?" he asked. We could see no reason why not, so we didn't answer.

We knew that there were many fine herds in Tennessee but this gentleman was advocating more herds and bigger herds. He said there were about 475 herds in this state that averaged around 18 head to make a total of approximately 8,400 in round numbers. This brought out his statement that there are about 568,000 in 13,200 herds throughout the country. These figures he gave as "cattle reported."

"The ultimate end of all beef cattle is the butcher's block. To be successful the producer must raise a quality of beef that is acceptable to the packer and satisfactory to the consumer," said the gentleman from Missouri. He added that Herefords "fill the bill."

Prolific Breed

There is always an overhead expense on a cow and unless she produces a calf every year she may become a liability rather than an asset. This we knew because Herefords are for beef and not for milk.

Kinzer pointed out that Hereford cows produce a larger calf crop because they will go farther and search longer for food, consequently they are thriftier. He said a thin cow is slower to breed than one in good flesh. Hereford cows make better mothers because they have that innate instinct to go the limit to find food and water—"they're not lazy," in other words. Calves of this breed inherit the hardiness and constitutions of their sires and dams and are better able to survive unfavorable treatment. "Good treatment insures more calves reaching maturity or 'marketing stage'" we were told.

Summed up he said, "Hereford sires insure the breeding of cows, the cows are better able to take care of their calves and the calves themselves are sufficiently vigorous to survive far more than average adversity."

The ability of an animal to stamp its likeness on its off-spring is a factor not to be overlooked. Failure to transmit those characteristics to its young would make the best herd of no avail.

"The unerring prepotency of the Herefords to reproduce their kind has contributed greatly to their popularity," said Kinser. "No matter what the degree of breeding of the scrub, grade or purebred cattle with which they are crossed, the calves uniformly bear the characteristic whiteface and desirable qualities of the breed," he stated. Buyers of feeder, fat, or purebred cattle are attracted by the uniformity, size, and quality of the Hereford. This "adds dollars and cents to their value and produces a more salable product."

Market Toppers

Records of the Chicago market show that Herefords top the market regularly, according to Kinser. "Ninety-two days out of 104 regular market days during the first six months of 1941 show that Hereford steers were tops on this market and averaged 97 pounds heavier than other market-topping steers. And fifty out of 78 loads reported for yearly tops (Chicago market) from 1887 to 1940 were Herefords," he said. Furthermore, there has only been one load in the last ten years, that was in 1938, that was not Herefords in the yearly top cattle sales on the market at Chicago, he added.

Early Maturity

With the decrease in acreage of range lands, the high price of concentrated feeds and the present and ever-increasing demand for small cuts of beef, the importance of an early maturing breed of cattle is not to be overlooked.

That's where the Hereford is tops again, according to Kinzer who said the well-established characteristic of maturing at an early age makes them popular with the feeder and the packer.

In the days of plentiful range land it made but little difference whether beef cattle matured in two or five years. Then beef was cheap and the average housewife bought a goodly-sized piece of beef steak, the choice part of which was served on the table and the rest disposed of as waste.

"Today there is a different story. Much range land has been cut into small farms and when these produce cattle the prices are high. The modern housewife wants a small cut that will give the family a sufficient portion and leave nothing to be wasted," Kinzer avowed. He added that, for these reasons, many feeders are paying a premium for calves or feeders that show a preponderance of Hereford blood.

Economical

Economy of production is of vast importance in determining the best breed of beef cattle. If a manufacturing plant turned out an article that met the demands of the public but could not place it on the market at a profit to the owners there would be no incentive for the establishment to stay in business.

"So it is with the manufacturer of beef," said Kinzer who stated that the Hereford can be fattened at any age profitably. Further along this important line he added, "Suffice it to say that the easy-fattening qualities, combined with the docile disposition and early maturity, has made the Hereford the favorite of all beef animals with producers and feeders of cattle wherever found."

When we told him that we believed more Herefords on more hills and in more fields throughout Middle Tennessee would add to the beauty of the land and to the profits of the farmers, he said this without hesitation: "If you want beauty just take into consideration the Hereford color combination which is a badge of purity and courage—white, the symbol of purity; red, the mark of courageous strength. And remember that Herefords are the breed which has changed the complexion of our feed lots and whitewashed the faces of the cattle on a thousand hills—so why not more Herefords on your Middle Tennessee farms?"

Feeding the hogs.

A field of shocked wheat.

Standing wheat ready to harvest.

Inspecting the tall corn.

MAURY COUNTY REMEMBERED

Checking the grain.

TOP
Tobacco buyers.

BOTTOM
*Maury County
Tobacco
Warehouse.*

Tobacco ready
for sale.

MAURY COUNTY REMEMBERED

THIS PAGE
Grand Champion
Bull of the
National Dairy
Show, 1941.

OPPOSITE
This Holstein herd
set a national
record for milk
production in
May, 1940.

Sheep with wool to be sheared.

Mule Day at Halliday Farm on Campbellville Pike.

"Lex Watson, Billy Alderson, Gillie Mac Orr, and a miniature mule."

The Gilbert MacWilliams Orr Collection

Billy Alderson holding a minia-ture mule.

MAURY COUNTY REMEMBERED

Young lady feeding Dominecker chickens.

Tending hogs on the farm.

*Maury County
farm scenes.*

THIS PAGE
and
OPPOSITE
*Maury County
farm scenes.*

HORSES AND
HORSE SHOWS

5

THE TENNESSEE WALKING HORSE

Maury County is in that small area of the United States where the Tennessee Walking Horse has flourished for more than a century. In no other part of the world are these much-sought-after saddle animals in such abundance as this section of Middle Tennessee which was largely settled by those who came across the mountains from Virginia and the Carolinas, many of whom brought their horses with them.

The Thoroughbred stallions of these early settlers were mated with mares whose blood did not class them as high as the male progenitors. As the colts of these stallions came along with enough finish and spirit to satisfy the public, and with the docility, ease of action and varied gaits of their dams—the Tennessee Walking Horse came into its own.

This horse is now sought from all parts of the country by those who want a sturdy and durable saddle animal for pleasure riding and for long distance travel, one which has a technique of movement all its own. General Andrew Jackson in 1790 wrote to a friend about a horse called Free and Easy—"As was his name, so was his gait," said Old Hickory in speaking of this particular type of saddle horse.

Today these horses are about 15 1/2 hands in average size. They have clean bone and much muscle, sound feet,

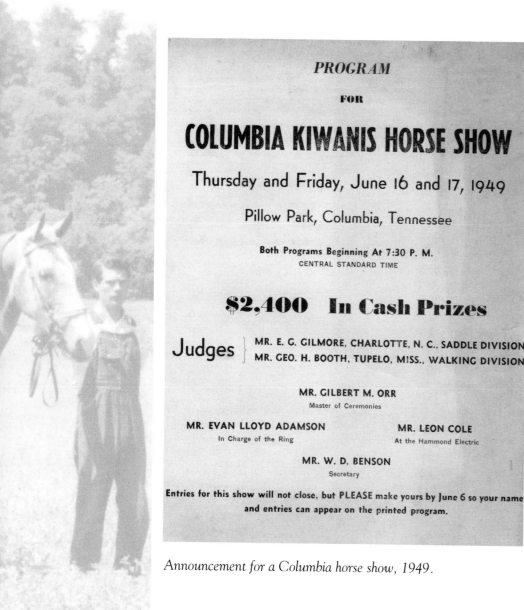

PROGRAM

FOR

COLUMBIA KIWANIS HORSE SHOW

Thursday and Friday, June 16 and 17, 1949

Pillow Park, Columbia, Tennessee

Both Programs Beginning At 7:30 P. M.
CENTRAL STANDARD TIME

$2,400 In Cash Prizes

Judges } MR. E. G. GILMORE, CHARLOTTE, N. C., SADDLE DIVISION
MR. GEO. H. BOOTH, TUPELO, MISS., WALKING DIVISION

MR. GILBERT M. ORR
Master of Ceremonies

MR. EVAN LLOYD ADAMSON   MR. LEON COLE
In Charge of the Ring   At the Hammond Electric

MR. W. D. BENSON
Secretary

Entries for this show will not close, but PLEASE make yours by June 6 so your name
and entries can appear on the printed program.

Announcement for a Columbia horse show, 1949.

thin necks, and sloping shoulders, with backs and loins of great strength. They are known for their good dispositions, and are game with gentleness. For those who do not want a horse for his rough and fast gaits, this animal is ideal for much use and great pleasure.

The walking horse has three gaits—the flat-foot walk, the running-walk, and the canter. The movement is one of continual breaking over from a walk to that which is faster, accompanied by a pushing that makes for a long stride. A good walking horse often takes strides so long as to overlap by as much as eighteen inches the track of the forefoot by the pushing hind foot. The gait is so easy on both the horse and the rider that it may be continued for hours without fatigue.

When this animal starts "walking" he is best when fully relaxed. Then his head nods, his ears flop in rhythm, and his teeth may even clatter against the bit—a movement so easy that the rider might carry a glass of water on his head without spilling a drop as the horse "walks" along. The peculiar nod of the head when this animal is in action, a nod with each stride of the running-walker, is a sight of beauty to him or her who loves a saddle horse. These gaits are so natural to a well–bred walking horse that it is not an uncommon sight to see a foal before it is weaned follow its dam with all the gaits of an older and a trained horse.

The Tennessee Walking Horse abounds in and around Columbia in many colors; however, most are sorrel, black, and roan. Some are pure white, and a few are yellow with white mane and tail.

For pleasurable and healthful exercise, and for sheer joy of riding, this animal affords a maximum of satisfaction and benefit. His variety of uses, his docility and ease of handling, his affectionate yet courageous nature, together with his smoothness of action and length of gait makes him the "gentleman of the equines" and the superb saddle and pleasure horse of the world.

THE TENNESSEE PACER

The fame of Maury County's Mules and that of her Walking Horses may exist by dint of their own merit before a public which is either lavish in praise or harsh in criticism; but, by all standards of right, the glorious history of the Tennessee Pacer which flourished here in another day (and whose blood strains still dot the countryside), is a stepping stone to whatever heights of greatness the mule and the saddle horse may attain.

It was here that the first horses ever to negotiate a mile under harness in less than two minutes was bred and trained, Star Pointer 1:59 1/4. It was here that Walter Direct 2:05 3/4, one of the world's greatest sires, was foaled and added glory to the turf. This was true of Napoleon Direct 1:59 3/4, a son of Walter Direct, who beat the great Single G in most of the starts against him. Both of these famous horses were handled by the immortal Ed "Pop" Geers, and today their homes are dust in the bluegrass acres of Maury County.

A son of Napoleon Direct is today the champion pacer of the world, Billy Direct 1:55, who established his record at Lexington, Kentucky in September 1938 when he clipped one-fourth of a second off the mark of Dan Patch which had stood fro 35 years—and Billy Direct travelled in the open without benefit of windshield or breaker!

One of the greatest pacing mares of history was Grace Direct 2:00 1/2, a daughter of Walter Direct. This Maury County mare was on the grand circuit from 1918 through

Prize-winning roadster bike.

1926, and out of 111 starts won 74, was second 19 times, third 3 times, fourth 8 times, and in her entire career failed to place only 7 times. This record has never been equalled by any other pacing mare. She died in 1935 at the age of 21 years.

Coming from the Copperbottoms and the Thoroughbreds, the pacer has shed lustre in the racing world. Dating from the days before the Civil War, many fine horses have lived here. McMeen's Traveller was one of the greatest sires of saddle horses which this section of the South has known. His gets were many and great—they were the foundation stock of the finest blood that continues to flow in many parts of the land today. This Maury County stallion's pedigree is traced back to the immortal Lexington. Gibson's Old Tom Hal was a famous stallion here at the close of the War between the States.

With the coming on in 1879 of Brown Hal 2:12 1/4, the Hal family was definitely established. This great horse was owned by Maj. Campbell Brown and Capt. M. C. Campbell at Ewell's Station in Maury County where he was kept in stud after a career on the grand circuit in which he was never beaten, and in which he established his record in his last start when Ed "Pop" Geers held the reins.

Some famous gets of Brown Hal were Star Pointer 1:59 1/4; Argot Hal 2:04 3/4 pacing and 2:07 1/4 trotting, at one time the champion double-gaited horse of the world; Hal Dillard 2:04 3/4; and Hal Akin 2:05 3/4. So much for the Hal family of Maury County.

Here in 1891 at the old kite-shaped track near Columbia Geers drove Hal Pointer 2:04 3/4 in the now famous race against Direct 2:05 1/2 from California. From this race the course of pacing history took a sudden turn which has lead to the world's record of today. For in this race Direct beat the great Hal Pointer. Geers, a genius in the matter of horses, was quick to see that the stamina of the Hals crossed with the speed of Direct would produce an

Brood mares with colts.

unbeatable strain. The correctness of his judgment has been amply proven. Direct could dart like an arrow, and the gameness and sheer strength of Hal Pointer could not be equaled—hence, the vision of Geers.

Bessie Hal by Gibson's Tom Hal was bred to Direct, the get being Direct Hal 2:04 1/4, a horse which was never beaten. When Direct Hal met Ella Brown 2:11 1/4, a mare as game as any which ever lived, the foal was Walter Direct, sire of Napoleon Direct, sire of Billy Direct.

Other famous horses of the Direct family which were foaled in Columbia and Maury County, or whose blood strains are traced directly here, were Merry Direct, sire of Winnepeg 1:57 1/4; Kenny Direct 1:59; Napoleon Grant 2:00; Flower Direct 2:00 3/4; and Her Ladyship 1:56 3/4, out of La Paloma by Walter Direct. So much for the Direct family of Maury County.

Columbians and Maury Countians who have been prominent in the history of the Tennessee Pacer are Dr. W. P. Woldridge, Allen Campbell and Robert M. Williams, all of whom are living today. Major Campbell Brown, Capt. M. C. Campbell, Ed Geers, A. W. McKay, Smith Thomas, John McGaw, W. J. Webster, Jr., William M. and Frank Chaffin, and W. M. and Joe Tolley have all passed on the turf's Valhalla from "The Dimple of the Universe."

HORSES AND MULES

Last week we gave you a portion of a letter that a practical farmer in Illinois, Mr. A. L. Goodenough of Morrison, wrote to Wayne Dinsmore, secretary of the Horse and Mule Association of America at Chicago.

This Illinois farmer had been reluctant to talk, but he turned it on when "desk farmers" and others had tried to preach the horse to oblivion on the farm.

He continues, and this part of his letter is quite appropriate at this time of the year:

A lady riding side saddle wrote:
"This is the way I did it."

A Team Pulls Them Out of the Mud

"Another neighbor of mine got stuck last fall with his tractor and corn picker in a wet spot in the field. Another neighbor ran down with his tractor, but he too got mired. It took just one team of good horses to haul the whole bunch out of the mud.

"Last spring, on one of my farms, the pump broke down. There is about a half mile of gravel road leading to the farm. It was impossible to travel this road at the time with a car or truck, but the team of horses hitched on in front pulled the pump repair man, with his truck and load of tools, through mud and slush axle deep, to the farm and out again, making a bad situation comparatively simple.

"My cattle yard is not all cement. It is situated on a side hill. The cattle shed is of course up on the high side, and it gets pretty soft and deep in the spring or during any mild winter weather for twenty or thirty feet in front of the shed. But my team takes a load of bedding to the shed in any kind of weather—mud or deep snow. I couldn't get half way there with my tractor.

"We thresh our grain in this neighborhood, not because we have never heard of a combine but because we consider threshing better suited to our needs. We have a good threshing outfit. Ten adjoining farms have help enough to do the job nicely, putting the grain in the bin and straw in the barn or stack in one operation—and doing it better, cheaper, and with less risk than any other way. And we all have a team of horses to haul the bundle wagons.

Extra Helpers and a Machine to Do a Two-Horse Job

"Does anything look sillier than a sight I saw this summer? They were hauling bundles to the thresher with six wagons, three of which were pulled by horses and three by tractors. It was necessary to have an extra helper to drive each tractor—starting and stopping forty or fifty times with each load, and using a 12 or 15-horse tractor and an extra man to do a two-horse job. Yet it is said we farmers are becoming more and more efficient every day. Oh! Yeah!

"Last year I kept a team of mares and their weanling foals in the barn at night, and when not in use they were turned in a yard by the barn and had access to a rack of hay. At night they were fed a light feed of grain. I kept the team around the barn because I needed them for something every day or so, and I tied up their foals to get them halter broken and used to being handled.

"This spring I hauled out twenty manure-spreader loads of manure from this team of mares and their foals, made during the winter in the barn and around the feed rack in the yard.

"According to records kept by different universities, at the present value of feeds and fertilizers, manure (with bedding in it) has a fertilizing value of from $2.50 to $5.00 per ton. This will go a long way toward reducing the feed cost of wintering a team of horses.

Horses Came through Winter in Fine Condition

"My other horses spent the winter in a timber pasture where there was shelter from the cold winds and a water supply that was never frozen over. Those horses came through in fine condition. A team of young horses so treated is daily developing more efficiency and value. While the tractor may not be eating, it is daily decreasing in value, producing no fertilizer, and doing nothing toward reproducing itself.

"Mules cannot be produced without mares, and someone must produce the mares. The logical place to do that is on the farms of the Corn Belt, where tons and tons of unmarketable horse feed are going to waste every year—feed which a team of horses would be glad to convert into energy and fertilizer if given a chance.

"The sad part of it is that the younger generation is being drawn away from the horse by the lure of the tractor seat. They are losing their love of farm animals, especially horses, because it takes a little time to do the horse chores. They want to come to the house, jump off the tractor seat, eat supper, and get into the car and go places.

"But times are sure to change, and instead of thinking only 'Is it easier and will it save me any time and sweat' we are going to think in terms of economy and efficiency. We will ask ourselves, 'Will it save me money and do as good a job with a smaller investment of less expense in upkeep?'

How Good a Team of Horses or Mules Will Look Then

"When our corn cribs, oat bins and hay-mows are bulging with feed and no market for it, and our pocket books and gas barrels are empty, and the old tractor goes limping along, steadily getting worse and giving no signs of producing another of its kind, then—how good a team of horses or mules will look to us!

J. L. Haynes riding The G–Man.

"And remember that that time will come just as sure as day follows night. Some will be prepared for it; others will not.

"It is just too bad that horses are not born three years old, well broken, with harness on and with more sense than most university graduates are expected to have. But they are not. They are just like all the rest of God's creations—they are diamonds in the rough.

"Every horse muscle is so placed as to produce the greatest possible efficiency; their backs for carrying or pulling heavy loads, their shoulders so shaped that a collar can be placed there without producing friction, and a place left in the mouth, where there are no teeth, for a bit so that the horse may either eat or drink even when some thoughtless driver neglects to remove the bit.

Ready for a Life of Service

"The horse has just enough intelligence to make it possible for a human being to control him. If he had any more, he would not let anyone handle him; if he had any less, he could not be taught what we require and expect of him.

"The horse comes into this world ready to begin his life of service. Within an hour he shows an inclination and determination to get something to eat, if there is anything of that nature around—and the Wise Creator fixed that matter for him. This trait of seeking food stays with him throughout his life; but he is willing and able to give value received when man furnishes his feed.

"Ever ready to convert farm roughage into energy and valuable fertilizer, and ever ready to do his part toward producing food for millions, let's give the horse his rightful place on every farm (and it is not a real honest-to-goodness farm without him) where God intended that he should be."

HORSE SHOWS

Fame of State's Walking Horses Will Be Spread by Exhibitions

The big blue and white van from Haynes Haven Stock Farm at Spring Hill left here today en route to Pittsburgh, Pa., where the fame of the Tennessee Walking Horse will be spread throughout that section of the East in two exhibitions there Saturday and Sunday.

The cargo, bearing The G-Man and Greater Glory, will be augmented at Brentwood where Southern Colonel from Maryland Farm will be loaded for the trip and for the exhibition at South Park, Pittsburgh. The show there July 4 and 5 is to be sponsored by the Board of County Commissioners of Allegheny County and will be held under the supervision of the South Park Matinee Club.

Accompanying the van were Billy Grubbs from Haynes Haven Stables who will ride Greater Glory, and Bill Brewer from the Maryland Farm Stables who will be up on Southern Colonel in the two exhibitions.

Col. J. L. Haynes of Spring Hill and J. Truman Ward of Brentwood will leave their mid-state farms Thursday night by train to meet their horses at Pittsburgh. Colonel Haynes will be in the saddle on The G-Man when the exhibition of the "free and easy" gaits is given in the steel capital of America. Ward will be at the mike of the public address system as these horses show the Easterners the flatfoot walk, the running walk, and the canter.

Instrumental in having these Tennessee Walking Horses at Pittsburgh for this exhibition is L. A. Dixon, Jr., owner of Walkaway Farms at DuBois, Pa., where he has Pride of Smithville No. 380061, eight-year-old stallion by Ed Nowlin F-8, at stud. Dixon was elected a member of the Tennessee Walking Horse Breeders' Association of America at the annual meeting at Lewisburg, last May.

In the van also were Crown of Glory and Lindy Lou Allen from Haynes Haven Stock Farm which were taken along at the request of Dixon in order that horse fanciers around Pittsburgh "might see more Tennessee Walking Horses." And the remainder of the cargo

Saturn, a Walking Horse colt, at Haynes Haven.

was 10,000 folders which will be distributed among spectators at the two big shows.

The G-Man No. 410415 is a six-year-old chestnut gelding by Wilson's Allen 350075 and out of Lady Kidd by Ramsay's Frank Allen by Jim Allen by Roan Allen F-38. He is winner of many championships in Tennessee and will make his debut in the East Saturday night.

Greater Glory No. 380367 is a four-year-old chestnut mare by Wilson's Allen and out of Mary Allen by Hunter's Allen F-10 by Allan F-1. She has had a phenomenal and meteoric career and her championship wins are many. After winning the mare class at the Tennessee Walking Horse National Celebration at Shelbyville last September her overstep of 24 inches attracted the attention of Life Magazine which ran her picture in a fall issue.

Southern Colonel No. 400959 is a two-year-old strawberry roan stallion which has just been placed under the saddle this season. He is young but is of splendid conformation and his gaits are such that knowing horsemen expect him to go far afield in the show arena before he is retired to the stud.

When The G-Man, Greater Glory, and Southern Colonel give this exhibition at Pittsburgh this weekend it will mark the second appearance in the East of the Tennessee Walking Horse, now called a "natural resource" of the state. Their first appearance was at Madison Square Garden in New York City in November, 1939, where a dozen individuals were sent by the Tennessee Walking Horse Breeders' Association of America, and where they were hailed for their "free and easy" gaits and were heralded in the press as "the world's greatest pleasure horse."

LEFT
Billie Grubbs riding Greater Glory.

RIGHT
Bill Brewer riding Southern Colonel.

Scenes from the Tennessee Walking Horse National Celebration.

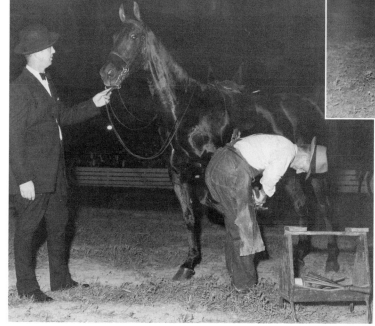

Walking horses at Haynes Haven.

MAURY COUNTY REMEMBERED

*Midnight Sun—
national
champion.*

LEFT
Melody's Heir.

RIGHT
Delina Boy.

The Gilbert MacWilliams Orr Collection

MAURY COUNTY REMEMBERED

MULES AND
MULE DAY FESTIVITIES

6

THE HYBRID OF THE ANIMAL KINGDOM

The mule is a very ancient and a right honorable member of the animal kingdom, alebit this hybrid is frequently called a "jarhead," and a "burrtail," and is made the butt of jokes by those who know him not.

In the Book of Genesis we are told that Anah found the mules in the wilderness as he fed the asses of Zibeon, his father. We are likewise informed that it was a mule upon which Absalom, the rebellious son of David, was riding when his locks were caught in the branches of a tree and he was suspended between heaven and earth. In order to do honor unto Solomon when he was to be crowned King, David ordered that he be seated upon his own mule.

It is said that mules were shown at the ancient fairs at Tyre; and frequently a man was measured in worth by a mule—two-mule value.

There were no mules or horses, neither were there asses, in America at the time it was discovered by Columbus; but we are told that jacks were held out for public service in Virginia before the War of the Revolution.

It is well established that George Washington produced mules commercially at his Mt. Vernon farm in the year 1786 and following. It was in that year that John Fairfax, the

General's overseer, advertised Royal Gift for service. This advertisement appeared in a Philadelphia newspaper.

"Royal Gift" was a present to General Washington from the King of Spain. This jack was bred to the mares at Mt. Vernon and mules were produced which are said to have sold for as much as $200 per head.

Clyde Harlan and two prize mules.

Mules are the produce of the male donkey or ass bred to the female horse or mare.

The genealogy of a mule has been facetiously given in this manner: "The papa is the jackass. The mama is the mare. The papa's mama is the jennet. The mama's papa is the stallion. That makes the papa's mama its maternal grandfather. The paternal grandmother may be the sister or the daughter or the mother of its papa, and the maternal grandfather may be the brother or the son or the father of its mama.

"The question then becomes, what kin, if any, are its female forbears; and what degree of relationship, if any, exists between its male ancestors?"

The mule may be an animal "without pride of ancestry or hope of posterity," but breeders continue to produce these hybrids by crossing the jack on the mare—the mule cannot reproduce its kind, of course.

The mechanical age has been singing the swan song of the mule for a long time; but the mule is not down and out today, not by a long shot. The USDA, in its estimates of mules and colts on the farms of the country for 1946, said there were (as of January 1 of that year) 3,196 thousand head with a value of 420,556 thousand dollars. Of this number, Tennessee had 279,000 head of mules and mule colts with a value of $130 average for each head.

The mule is still a valuable and an almost indispensible adjunct to well-ordered agriculture, especially in the sections of the country where tractors and other motorized implements are not practical because of the topography or lay of the land. Mules are handy for various jobs about the farm, the truth of which will be readily admitted by any honest farmer.

Mules today are classified according to weight when sold on the market. The individuals weighing from 900 to 1,000 pounds up to 1,100 or 1,150 are called "cotton" mules and are sold to farmers and plantation owners in the cotton-producing sections of the country. Those which weigh from 1,150 to 1,300 or more are called "sugar" mules and are used in the sugar cane-growing sections where the soil is deep and black and heavy and where a big mule is needed for the work to be performed.

A mule should have a big and long head with bony face, long ear, short neck, short back and short legs. He should be muscular and his feet should have dense bone. The coat of the mule, or the hair, should be soft and satin-like. Dark colored mules with "mealy" points (white on nose tip and around eyes and under the belly) are most sought after, but sorrel mules are in good demand.

The mule inherits his head and ears and small feet, together with his stiff mane and tail, from the jack. In other matters of conformation he is not very different from his dam, the mare.

Other characteristics, aside from conformation or physical makeup, of the mule are quite different from those of

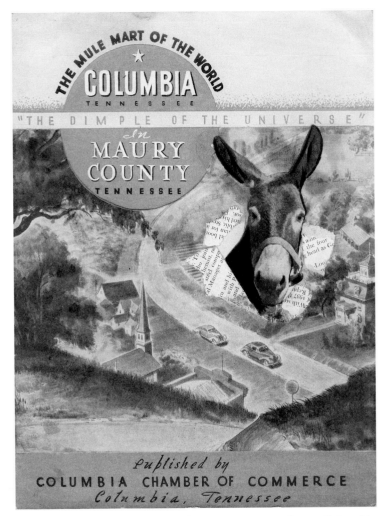

This Mule Day poster proclaims Columbia "Mule Mart of the World."

the horse. A mule is sure of foot, this coming from the jack. A mule will not run away and hurt himself, whereas a horse will injure himself by striking objects in his pathway. A mule may be turned into a stable or stall where there is an abundance of feed. He will eat whatever amount he wants or whatever is necessary for his sustenance or appetite, then turn and walk away from the heap. A horse will eat until he founders.

It is said that "a white mule never dies." Have you ever seen a dead white mule?

A SPRING FESTIVAL TO THE LOWLY MULE

In the smallish town of Columbia, located forty-three miles due south of Nashville in the bluegrass section of Middle Tennessee, a celebration is held each first Monday in April which has to do with the son of the jackass, commonly called the mule.

Columbia is the county seat of Maury County which has been chanted in song and related in story as "The Dimple of the Universe." It is within the area of the Volunteer State that is known as "The Walking Horse Capital of the World"—but the MULE is king in this small town which is rated as having slightly more than 7,000 inhabitants.

On April 3 the eighth annual Mule Day will be observed in a gay and colorful manner. All motor vehicles are relegated to the discard and a parade of mules, jacks, jennets, stallions, mares, walking horses, draft animals, and ponies wind their way through the streets of the city while from 30,000 to 40,000 people applaud the show.

The origin of this day is lost in antiquity. It is known to be more than a hundred years old. Back a century ago the breeders would gather on this first Monday in April to show their sires. Later it became known as Livestock Day. Since 1930 it has been sponsored by the Columbia

King Mule and Court on his float.

Chamber of Commerce and is now known far and near as "Mule Day."

During the weekend preceding this gala event the town is a seething mass of mules and horses. They are trucked in, and led in and ridden in to be boarded in barns until Monday comes along for the big parade to begin. At eleven o'clock in the morning this two-mile-long motorless spectacle moves from the West down through the residential and business section where it is given to the nation by radio, newsreel, commercial pictures, and the metropolitan press.

This year, on April 3, the parade will be headed by a new spectacle—"A Thousand Girls on A Thousand Mules." The county has ten civil districts. Each district will furnish 100 girls and 100 mules. A substantial cash prize will be awarded the district having the best costume for riders and the greatest number of girl riders. The quality of the mule will not be considered in the judging, for any mule is King in Maury County.

Following this will be the show mules which will be led by darkies from the farms nearby. Then will come the mule on a float, drawn by other mules, to be crowned "King for a Day" in a special ceremony to take place in front of the reviewing stands where the Honorable Prentice Cooper, Governor of Tennessee, and members of his cabinet, together with other dignitaries, will be stationed. The jeweled crown will be placed on the head of the King by a young lady to be selected for her beauty in a county-wide contest.

The mules to wagons and buggies will follow. The jacks and jennets, the stallions and mares, and the draft animals

Mule Day Parade along West Seventh Street, 1940s.

will come next in the parade. A special section will be given over to the famous Tennessee Walking Horse. In this contingent will be 500 of these saddle animals with their nodding heads and "running walk." Ponies and comics will bring up the rear of the motorless moving show.

Afternoon is the time for judging all classes of livestock which were a part of the parade. Then come teas, golf, trips to points of historical interest, old-time fiddling contests, and street dances. It's a gala day for all the people. Evening brings on a more formal atmosphere when the Bachelor Club stages its annual Mule Ball. There the sons and daughters of the planters, the debs and the sub-debs gather for a dance where a live mule leads the grand march down the dance floor. When comes the dawn these gay dancers file out into the early light and go riding on a mule down to hotels and restaurants and clubs for a bit of breakfast, but not until hay and corn has been provided for the hybrid. It's a ceremony that's a part of Mule Day.

Since the late beloved Will Rogers said, "It's Maiden Lane for Diamonds, but it's Columbia, Tennessee, for Mules" this celebration in the early springtime has become an institution in the county from whence come the Lex Watson Miniature Mules, the Tennessee Walking Horses, and the Hals and Directs of pacing fame.

And Will was seldom wrong—for Columbia is "the largest street mule market in the world." From 16,000 to 20,000 of the long-eared hybrids are sold on the streets of the city each year for a sum in excess of $2,000,000.

Do you wonder that this smallish town honors the mule!

"HIP-POCKET MULES"

A mule no larger than an over-sized Great Dane or New Foundland dog is a novelty, even in Columbia, Tennessee, which has lifted itself out of the ruck with the breeding and marketing of from 16,000 to 20,000 long-eared hybrids to the tune of an annual income of more than $2,500,000.

This miniature mule is now a reality which came into being through the dream and vision of Lex Watson, Columbia citizen who comes from a long line of jack breeders, who had an idea that a real MULE would be a smarter and more attractive animal for circuses and shows, for riding academies and for mines than would the burro or the donkey.

As a result of this idea of Watson, Columbia can now boast of being the home of the only midget mule extant while it swells with pride in the knowledge that it is widely known as the "Largest Street Mule Market in the World."

For the benefit of those who are not entirely familiar with this generally thought of ungainly and unromantic long eared creature which has more than 6,000 of its species in Maury County which has about 35,000 inhabitants, let it be said that a mule is the foal of the jackass and the mare.

The average sized mule at birth weighs from 80 to 100 pounds and is from 38 to 42 inches tall. When two years old, it weighs from 1,000 to 1,600 pounds and stands in heighth at from 14 to 16 hands—a "hand" being 4 inches as measurement goes in the tallness, as it were, of mule and horseflesh.

When mules are two years old they are "broke" to enter into a long life of service to their owners. They work to a plow, wagon, buggy; all wheeled farming implements; and do right nobly as saddle animals.

Mules are brought to Columbia from the 3,000 farms of Maury County on the "First Monday" in each month of the year and sold on the streets there to the buyers from the South and other sections who seek the best in muleflesh. For the market, mules are classified by the breeders and the buyers as "sugar" and "cotton" mules—these being the two types that produce for Maury County the staggering sum of more than $2,500,000 annually in street sales at Columbia.

The "sugar" mule is one which is from 14.75 to 16 hands high and weighs from 1350 to 1600 pounds. His name comes from his being brought by planters of the deep South where he is taken to work in the black and heavy soil where sugar "grows." The "cotton" mule is sold to the planters in the Carolinas, Georgia, Alabama, and other southern sections to work in a lighter and sandier soil which produces the cotton crop.

A top sugar mule brings from $250 to $275 while a top cotton mule is worth from $225 to $250—but little difference in the price of "tops" in mules. That's why Maury County goes in for mule producing in a big way and why Columbia, on the "First Monday" of each April "pays homage to the mule."

This year more than 40,000 gathered from twenty states on April 4th and viewed the three-mile-long parade of 2,000 mules as it winded its way through the tree lined streets of Columbia. Mules were led and mules were ridden. On the back of a large black mule sat Tennessee's Governor Gordon Browning. But the presence of the state's chief executive was eclipsed by a 20 Mule Team which transported the cream of the crop, a three year old top bay cotton mule, to the reviewing stand where this mule was officially crowned "King for a Day" amid the plaudits of the crowd which had foregathered to do honor to the lowly hybrid.

Excitement on the streets before Mule Day.

Mary Leslie Anderson, a member of the Columbia Girls Cotillion Club, and her mule.

But this story is to deal with a brand new, smallish, stream-lined animal which is to be called the miniature mule. This is an angle which has never heretofore existed in the mule industry of a county which has produced large mules and sold them on the market for so many years that no one will dare say just when this traffic first began.

A miniature or midget mule is the outgrowth of an idea which was conceived by Lex Watson when he decided he would cash in on a few Shetland ponies on his Highland Stock Farms two miles southeast of Columbia. Watson had long dreamed of a miniature jack. He found one that was perfectly formed and that stood but 42 inches "in his stocking feet." This was a real jack of Maltese stock. He weighed but 325 pounds and was of the same conformation as those larger jacks which came from Spain in the

Admit The Bearer

MULE DAY REVIEWING STAND
Northwest Side Court House
COLUMBIA, TENN., APRIL 7, 1941

General Chairman

139 *This Admission Ticket Is Not Transferable*

ABOVE
A ticket to the Mule Day viewing stand, 1941.

RIGHT
Mule Day Centennial Celebration poster, 1940.

days of George Washington and which caused such a furor in the days of Senator Stiles Bridges of TVA antagonism.

Watson produced the small blue jack (the exact color of a Maltese cat) and brought him to his farm. There he bred him to the smallest mares of his Shetland stock. Now he has one miniature mule which is but five weeks old and stands but 26 inches tall. This fine young fellow weighs less than fifty pounds, but is "as playful as a kitten."

This first midget mule of Maury is out of Gregg's Black Beauty, a Shetland mare which is 41 inches tall, and by

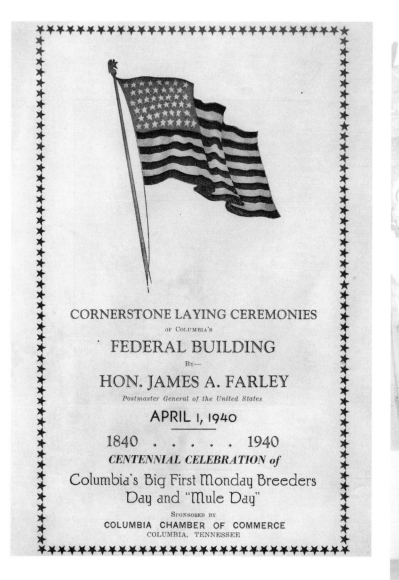

CORNERSTONE LAYING CEREMONIES
OF COLUMBIA'S

FEDERAL BUILDING
BY—

HON. JAMES A. FARLEY
Postmaster General of the United States

APRIL 1, 1940

1840 1940
CENTENNIAL CELEBRATION of
Columbia's Big First Monday Breeders
Day and "Mule Day"

SPONSORED BY
COLUMBIA CHAMBER OF COMMERCE
COLUMBIA, TENNESSEE

Souvenir

of

Columbia, Tennessee,

"Largest Street Mule

Market in the World."

25¢

ADMIT ONE
MULE DAY CIRCUS
Pillow Park, Columbia, Tenn.
MONDAY, APRIL 7, 1941
1:30 P. M.

Pulling Contest, Log Loading Contest, Steeple-chase and Running Races, Trick Riding, and Walking Mules under Saddle.

Sam and Kirk McGee and Their Boys From Tennessee, and Zeke Clements, "The Dixie Yodeler," artists from WSM Grand Ole Opery.

Sponsored by Columbia Chamber of Commerce

ADMISSION 15c

(Children under ten free when accompanied by parent or other paid admission.)

ABOVE
Ticket to the 1941 Mule Day Circus in Pillow Park.

LEFT
Souvenir program from Mule Day distributed by the Columbia Chamber of Commerce.

"Highland County," the tiny blue jack, whose name is appropriate of his habitat at Highland Stock Farms and his "singing voice"—as rich a "baritone" as that of his larger brethren of the jackass family.

"This is not a hinny," said Watson in speaking of his mule colt, "for a hinny is a sort of freak from the mule's paternal grandmother by the mule's maternal grandfather," he explained. To make it perfectly clear, he said a hinney was the foal of a mare and a jack makes it a MULE," Watson added.

The brood mares at Highland Stock Farms now number 60, and all the potential producers of miniature mules are under 42 inches in heighth. "I have selected the smallest Shetland mares I could find," Watson said, "but I have looked for quality while searching for smallness, for the mules I will produce are going to lose nothing the larger mules have except about 1200 pounds in weight," he added.

Fifteen other mares are now in heavy foal by Highland Canary. A few will drop a colt within a month, and many of his sons and daughters will be dropped in the spring of '39. "I am going to get a spotted mule," the veteran breeder said, "fancy mules bring fancy prices," he continued with a smile. "Orders for eight of these miniature mules have already reached me, and I have had visitors from Maryland and Ohio who come here in search of these midgets of the hybrid family," said Watson.

Mule breeders around Columbia say a foal is seldom larger than its sire or dam, so it is to be expected that the mules of Highland Farms will never grow to a heighth of more than 42 inches. This seems entirely reasonable to believe, for an ordinary mule colt at the age of this miniature youngster would be from 40 to 44 inches tall—and what is more it would weigh from 100 to 120 pounds. "Just remember that the first born son of my blue jack and my black mare is only 26 inches tall and tips the scales at less than fifty pounds today, which is the fifth week of his birth,"

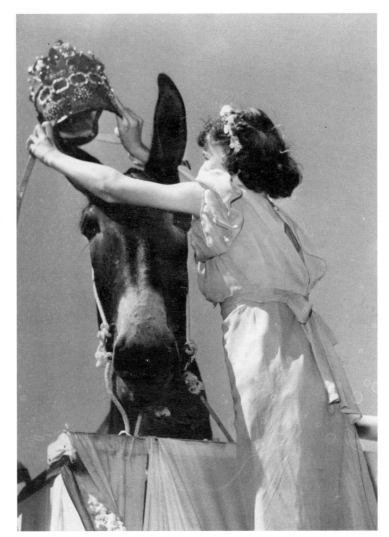

Crowning the King Mule.

said Watson, "and you can't figure it out where I will ever be able to class him as a sugar or cotton mule," he said.

Watson said he would receive from $75 to $100 for each midget mule he produced. "Not bad for so small a piece of muleflesh," he said with a twinkle in his eye, "and when I get that spotted mule colt, I can ask my own price," he added.

To say the least of it this mule breeder has something new under the sun; and with many letters coming to him each month inquiring about his tiny hybrids Watson believes he has started an industry that has potentialities for large expansion. "When you have the proper raw material and keep up the quality, your finished product is bound to be good and will always find a ready market," said Watson.

So while miniature mules are being produced at Highland Stock Farms near Columbia, the breeders of sugar and cotton mules that sell when they are 14 to 16 hands high and weigh from 1000 to 1600 pounds—these old boys are watching the new angle of their ancient trade and wondering what the 40,000 spectators who will gather on Mule Day next April will think of a section of the three-mile-long parade that is to be made up of "pocket-sized" mules.

"MULE DAY" AT COLUMBIA, TENNESSEE

When bands play and mules bray it's "Mule Day" at Columbia in the Middle Division of Tennessee where the hybrid of the animal kingdom has been a valuable worker in the field of agriculture for a century and more. The "First Monday" in April is his day, and after a lapse of six years this spring festival is coming back with all its glamour and glory.

The motorless parade will form and start its line of march down broad West Seventh Street at 11:00 A. M. on Monday, April 7. It will halt at the court square and the Hon. Jim McCord, governor of Tennessee, will hand the jeweled crown to the Mule Day Queen (a lovely girl from Maury County) who will place the diadem on the head of King Mule.

This mule, a splendid specimen, will be on a float drawn by six other mules; and riding with the King will be the Queen and the Ladies of her Court. This is the highlight of the day and the crown is that which has graced the heads of nine other "Kings," because Mule Day was inaugurated at Columbia by one W. D. Hastings in 1933. It was held annually until 1941 when it was discontinued for the duration of the war.

Mule Day is coming back now, not only with this motorless parade (which in the past has been sometime three miles long), but with the Mule Show, the Mule Circus, and the Mule Dance.

In the morning parade mules will be ridden under saddle and bareback; they will be lead to halter, and will be driven to four-wheeled vehicles; they will be long and short, old and young, slick and shiny, and marked with harness and traces. The braying of the hybrids will compete with the playing of the bands as thousands line the streets of this city that has a population of about 15,000 mule-loving citizens.

Following the parade a Mule Show will be held on the street in the business section. It's a holiday at Columbia when it's Mule Day. Classes for mules will be held according to ages and sex, and mules will be shown in hand in singles and in pairs. The Championship Mule Stake will select the Champion of the World at Columbia.

Then, at 2:30 P. M. will come the Mule Circus. There mules will compete in pairs in a pulling contest—a huge log from the forests dragged across the face of the good earth. A log loading contest will determine the pair of mules most amendable to the driver and most skillful in getting the log onto the wagon and tying it down in the shortest length of time.

Mules will enter a steeplechase over brush jumps, the riders going bareback on the hybrids. There will be "wild" mules which will be the media for riders to test their skill at staying aboard without benefit of surcingle. And there'll be a potato race on mules—mounting, riding, dismounting, picking up one potato, mounting, riding, dropping the spud in a bucket, and repeating. Hillbilly music and old-time fiddling will enliven the circus.

When evening comes there will be a square dance and a fiddling contest. Later a round dance of modern version, as it were, will hold sway until the wee small hours.

The whole day, from parade to final strains of the orchestra at the dance, is sponsored by the Columbia Chamber of Commerce, a live-wire body in the capital city of Maury County in "The Dimple of the Universe."

Each future Mule Day is an unknown in estimating the crowd that will attend. If past performance can be taken as a criterion, as it were, for the spectators who will mill about the city of Columbia on April 7, 1947, it is safe to say that upward to 50,000 persons will be present to honor the lowly son of the jackass—that's the number who watched with starry-eyed wonder as a thousand mules paraded there on the "First Monday" in April 1941 before Pearl Harbor plunged us into war.

THE MULE TROT

Originated in Columbia, Tennessee; premiere at Bachelor Club's Mule Ball on Mule Day, April 4th, 1938.

THE MULE TROT WAS BORN IN THE MINDS OF SOME OF the members of the Bachelor Club of Columbia from a desire to furnish entertainment that was different and that would be in keeping, as it were, with the occasion of Columbia's annual Mule Day.

Blake Campbell was the leading spirit in originating the Mule Trot. Mr. Campbell's dancing partner was Miss Sarah Anne Ridley. Other bachelors and their girls who ably assisted in creating and formulating steps of the Mule Trot were: Harry Hill Borum and Gale Armstrong, Van Shapard and Eleanor Roscher, Jimmy Dedman and Martha Stratton Sloan, Houston Crozier and Louise Scales. Mr. George L. Buchnau, member of the Bachelor Club, is probably the father of the dance, because it was at his suggestion that the Mule Trot came to being.

The Mule Trot is based upon the life, habits, and traits of the mule. The dance is done to rhythmic swing music in four-four time. The steps are in counts of four, and in as many counts as the leader desires the dancers to continue. The dance is called, that is to say the steps are done at the call of the leader.

The basic or theme step is a double tap jog which sounds very like the trot of a mule–hence the name. This theme step introduces the dance and is done between each special or called step.
The special steps are as follows:

PAW STEP—Boy and girl side by side, boy's right arm around girl's waist . . . her left arm around boy's waist . . .right foot reaches out and "paws" through the air to the floor, in the manner of mules when they are wont to paw.

PLOW STEP—Boy puts his hands behind him and holds them back to the girl who takes hold of them and "plows" the boy until the leader calls "Gee Mule," which is a command to turn to the right; the positions are then reversed with the boy "plowing" the girl until the leader calls "Haw Mule" and they then turn left.

BALK STEP—Boy and girl face each other, hold hands, pull backward from the waist line while the knees are bent in; a rhythmic "balk" just as the mule is sometimes wont to refuse to move (balk).

STOP THAT MULE—Boy stops, girl goes round him . . .

when she is in front of him she turns slightly to side, raises right foot and he takes it across his knee . . . they both go round as he beats a rhythmic tap on the bottom of her foot and "nails" the shoe.

MILLING AROUND—Just what the name implies—couples go round and round in wheels of eight while holding the hand to the inside or at hub of the wheel.

FEELING YOUR OATS—A quick, frisky movement in rhythmic step with head high, chest out, shoulders back, and knees moving "pump-like."

HEADED FOR THE FEED TROUGH—Boy's right arm around waist of girl, and her left arm around his waist—these arms being used to support body as each "rears back" . . . outside arms up, headback, knees up and down as they go off the floor-the dance is over; and thereby hangs a mule tale.

Leading the mule
to set the stage for
a square dance

A handsome mule
with pretty girls.
Left to right: Ann
Roach, Nita Goff,
Gwen Glass,
Katherine Dealy,
and June Garrett.

Maury County Remembered

THIS PAGE
*WSM announcers
riding double.*

OPPOSITE
*Women riders
waiting to join
the parade.*

Fancy attire at the Mule Day Parade.

MAURY COUNTY REMEMBERED

The Gilbert MacWilliams Orr Collection

*Old timers lined
up to watch the
festivities.*

THIS PAGE
Arriving in appropriate Mule Day fashion.

OPPOSITE
The media frenzy at Mule Day.

MAURY COUNTY REMEMBERED

AFTERWORD

Things I Love
by Gilbert MacWilliams Orr

Dawn on an October morning . . . the sound of horses' hoofs on a graveled road . . . the rushing roar of a train late at night . . . Brahms' Lullaby . . . smoke hanging near the ground in the autumn . . . the sight of a game fish leaping from the water . . . mimosa trees in bloom . . . rock chimneys . . . acres of crimson clover carpeting fields like a deep-red Persian rug . . . the smell of country ham frying . . . the far-away purr of an out-board motor . . . lettuce and roquefort salad . . . the chop of the woodman's axe sounding from deep within a forest.

The roll of iron-rimmed wagon wheels on cobble stones . . . the freshness of a new shave . . . operas by Verdi . . . the mountains of East Tennessee . . . grill-work on the gates at Charleston . . . blades of blue grass . . . the chatter of martins selecting a home in early spring . . . chess pies . . . the swift dart of a trout under clear water . . . Sousa's marches . . . the sight of Old Glory waving in the breeze . . . live oaks along the Gulf Coast . . . new neck-ties . . . the first frost of autumn . . . the 23rd Psalm.

The flight of gulls going out to sea . . . the evening star . . . trotting horses coming in on the home stretch . . . the drone of textile spindles . . . road runners running in Texas . . . honeycombed limestone rocks . . . the crack of a ball against a hard-swung bat . . . the creak of a new saddle and the smell of a new leather . . . country roads in New England . . . the song of a mockingbird on moonlit nights . . . the lake front at Chicago . . . the whir of partridge wings . . . cherry blossoms at Washington . . . the strut of a peacock.

The scream of a hawk at high noon . . . flowers that lift their faces to the warmth of the sunshine, and drop their

The rolling hills of Maury County.

heads in a shower of rain . . . the widening circle on still water caused by the drop of a pebble . . . a rainbow across the sky . . . the beauty of friendship . . . the ties that bind . . . the trait of loyalty in humankind . . . the comfort of "Lo, I am with you always" . . . sparks that fly upward from wood fires in the evenings of wintertime . . . sleep that gives rest in sweet oblivion.

Cool water that quenches burning thirst . . . cedar trees . . . the music of the masters . . . books by the sages of the ages . . . voices that blend in harmony . . . the peal of church bells . . . dew drops that cling to rose petals on misty mornings and sparkle at the touch of the sun . . . trees that stand as sentinels on mighty mountaintops.

Streams that run down to the sea . . . grains of sand that make the beach . . . the flash of lightning and the crash of thunder . . . the clean smell of the earth after a spring shower . . . glistening icicles that cling to bare twigs in the winter . . . words that comfort hurt hearts . . . holly and mistletoe and lighted candles and carols at Christmas . . . the sound of a gentle rain on a tin roof . . . embossed stationery that crackles when handled . . . new-plowed fields . . . clean cool sheets . . . the tinkle of a cow bell in a distant meadow as the evening comes silently on . . . little boys nine years old.

Night with its mystery . . . The moon riding high in the starstudded heavens . . . drifting clouds . . . the grandeur of nature . . . vast turbulent oceans . . . the majestic might of storms . . . gentle winds that kiss hot cheeks and cool fevered brows . . . ferns that grow in the mists by waterfalls

. . . wild flowers that shrink timidly in inaccessible places . . . the babble of a brook over clean pebbles in deep shaded nooks.

Footprints in the dew . . . the twitter of birds at dawn . . . the fragrance of newmown hay . . . fresh-peeled sticks . . . lambent flames that warm those who are cold . . . meteors streaking across the dome of the heavens when the earth is wrapped in darkness . . . the hush of eventide, and the boon of purple twilight . . . leaves that bud and grow green, turn red and yellow and brown, and then come tumbling down . . . squirrels that scamper across dry sticks in the fall.

The fluttering down of the first leaves that fall in autumn . . . home-made light bread . . . the honk of wild geese going South for the winter . . . the view from Mount Vernon . . . Talisman roses . . . water rippling and tumbling over rocks . . . the singing of a reel when a small-mouth black bass strikes and runs . . . the majestic beauty of the Rockies . . . the Episcopal twilight service during Holy Week . . . contact with keen minds . . . the thud of the punted pigskin, and the crack of a clean tackle.

The poetry of Keats and Shelley and Tennyson, and the delightful imagination of Coleridge . . . women who are brave . . . the roll of breakers coming in . . . evening dress . . . the loyalty of a dog for his master . . . quiet evenings with one who is congenial . . . the Book of Ruth and the Song of Solomon . . . the resonance of a lovely speaking voice . . . the colors of the spectrum . . . Margaret Mitchell's description of life at Tara and Twelve Oaks . . . the Lord's Prayer.

INDEX

Adams, John, 74
Alderson, Billy **107–8**
Allegheny County, Pa., 126
American Guernsey Cattle Club, 90
American Hereford Association, 91
American Revolution, 43, 53, 72, 139
Anderson, Mrs. C. D., 69
Anderson, Mary Leslie, **146**
Antrim, **80**
Armstrong, Charlotte (Mrs. Robert
    Wilson), 65–66
Armstrong, Gale, 152
Armstrong, James, 65–66
Arkansas, 54–55
Armour Fertilizer Works, 10
Armstrong Farm, 45
Ashwood Hall, 44, 47–48, **47,** 49–51, 54, 74
Aunt Jane (ex-slave), 63–64
Aunt Louise (cook), 86
Bachelor Club, 144, 152

Baroness de Charette. *See* Polk,
    Antoinette
Barrow, John D., 66
Barrow, Mrs. John D., 66–67
Barrow Place. *See* Wilson Place
Beecher, Henry Ward, 63
Bethel, William Decatur, 57
Bethel Hotel, **24**
Bethel Place, 57–59
Birmingham, Ala., 69, 74
Birmingham Division (L & N), 7
Bluegrass Warehouse, 88
Blythe Place, **73**
Booker, James Gray, 68
Booker, Mary (Mrs. Britton Drake
    Clopton), 68
Borum, Harry Hill, 152
Branch, Annie, 54
Branch, Joseph, 54
Brentwood, Tenn., 126

Brewer, Bill, **129**
Bridges, Stiles, 147
British, 45
Bronx Park, New York City, 63
Brown, Aaron V., 54
Brown, Campbell, 122–23
Brown, Granville Pillow, 54
Brown, Mary (Mrs. Harry Yeatman), 47
Browning, Gordon, 145
Buchanan, James, 54
Buchnau, George L., 152
Buena Vista, 44, 48
California, 122
Campbell, Allen, 123
Campbell, Blake, 152
Campbell, Elizabeth (Mrs. Absolom
    Thompson), 70
Campbell, M. C., 122–23
Campbell farm. *See* George Campbell farm
Campbellsville Pike, 58, 65, **105**

Carmack, Edward Ward, 24
Carolinas, 6, 119
Central Christian Church, **77**
Chaffin, Frank, 123
Chaffin, W. M., 123
Chaires. *See* Cheairs, Nathaniel
Chapel of the Polks. *See* St. John's
    Episcopal Church
Charleston Mining & Manufacturing
    Company, 10
Cheairs, Benjamin, 72
Cheairs, Elijah, 72
Cheairs, Mary Leonora (Mrs. James
    Turner Sanford Thompson, 71
Cheairs, Nathaniel, 72–73
Cheairs, Nathaniel, II, 72
Cheairs, Nathaniel, III, 73
Cheairs, Nathaniel, IV, 73–74
Cheairs, Sophie, 72
Cheairs, Susan McKissack, 73–74

Cheairs, Thomas, 72
Cheairs, Vachel, 72
Cheairs, William, 74
Cheairs Place, **72**, 74
Cheatham, Olive (Mrs. Granville
    Pillow), 59
Chickasaw Indians, 57
Chicago, Ill., 93, 123, 168
Churchill, Winston, 47
Cincinnati, Ohio, 51, 62
Cincinnati to New Orleans line (L & N),
    7, 27
Civil War, 6, 43–44, 48–52, 54, 58–59,
    63, 70–71, 73, 122
Cleburne, Patrick, 74
Clifton Place, 55–59
Clopton, Britton Drake, 68
Clopton Place, 69
Clover Bottom farm, 69
Columbia, Tenn., 5–8, 11–12, 21–22,
    24–28, 44–45, 47–48, 50, 53–55,
    60–61, 65–67, 69, 74, 88, 120, 122,
    141, 142, 145–46, 150–52
Columbia Athenaeum Rectory, **34**
Columbia Chamber of Commerce,
    142–43, **148**, 151
Columbia Division (L & N), 8
Columbia Fire Department, **33**
Columbia Girls Cotillion Club, **146**
Columbia Highway, 73
Columbia Institute, Episcopal School for
    Girls, 25, **25**, 48
Columbia Livestock Market, 23
Columbia Military Academy, 25–27, **26**,
    44
Columbia Police Department, **33**
Columbia Power System, 21
Commodity Credit Corporation, 88
Confederacy, 48–49, 69, 74
Confederates (Army), 49, 54, 59, 74
Cooper, Prentice, 143
Crozier, Houston, 152
Culleoka, Tenn., 8
Cumberland River, 52–54
Dale, Mrs. Andrew, 66

Dale, Elvira. *See* Pillow, Elvira Dale
Davidson County, Tenn., 52, 68
Davis, Paul M., 74
Dealy, Katherine, **155**
Dean Marble Company. *See* W. M. Dean
    Marble Company
Dedman, Jimmy, 152
Devereaux, Frances (Mrs. Leonidas
    Polk), 48
Dinning, John H., 69
Dinsmore, Wayne, 123
Diocese of Louisiana, 48
Diocese of Tennessee, 50
Dixon, L. A., Jr., 127
Donelson, Emily, 46
Du Bois, Pa., 127
Duck River, 23
Eastin, Mary (Mrs. Lucius Polk), 45–47
East Tennessee, 167
Edwards, Johnathan, 48
Elmwood, 54
England, 53
English Channel, 90
Ewell's Station, 122
Fain, Dr., 66
Fain, Eliza Wilson, 66
Fairfax, John, 139
Fairmount, 67–69, **67**
Federal Chemical Company, 10
Federals (Army), 54, 71, 74
Ferguson Hall, **79**
First Presbyterian Church, **36**
Fleming, Rebecca (Mrs. John Wilson), 66
Florida, 72
Forrest, Nathan Bedford , 71
Fort Donelson, 74
France, 64
Franklin, Tenn., 56, 70, 74
Garrett, June, **155**
Geers, Ed "Pop," 24, 121, 123
George Campbell farm, **90**
George Williamson Camp, **76**
Gist, States Rights, 74
Glass, Gwen, **155**
Goff, Nita, **155**

Goodenough, A. L., 123
Granberry Farm, 45
Granbery, Joseph J., 52
Granbury, Hiram, 74
Gray Farm, 45
Graymere Country Club, 24, **38**
Greene, Cornelia (Mrs. Peyton
    Skipwith), 60
Greene, Nathaniel, 60, 65
Grubbs, Billy **129**
Guernsey Island, 90
Gulf Coast, 167
Hagerstown, Md., 67
Halliday, William Parker, 56
Halliday, Mrs. William Parker, 60
Halliday Farm, **105**
Hamilton Place, 44–47, **46**, 48, 51–52
Hampshire, Tenn., 8
Hargill, Tex., 72
Harlan, Allen, 61–62
Harlan, Mrs. Allen, 62
Harlan, Ben, 61–62
Harlan, H. L., family, **60**
Harris, Isham G., 70
Hasting, W. D., 150
Hatton, General, 65
Hatton, Mamie, 65
Haynes, J. L., **125**, 126
Haynes Haven Stock Farm, 126–27,
    127, 132
Henderson, William A., 6
Highland Stock Farms, 146, 148–50
Hill Hurst Farm, 63
Hilliard, Mary (Mrs. George Polk), 51
Holland, James, 63
Holland, Winifred Sanford, 63
Holy Cross, 50
Hood, John Bell, 70–71, 73
Hoover & Mason, 10
Horse and Mule Association of America,
    123
Houston, P. D., 74
Hughes, D. R., 90
Humphries, West E., 54
India, 64

International Agricultural Corporation, 10
Ireland, 69
Jackson, Andrew, 5, 45–47, 53, 119
Jackson College, 64, 71
Jackson Highway, 65
James K. Polk Gardens, **44**
James K. Polk Home, **42, 45**
Jewell, Charles Worthington, 56
Johnston, Albert Sidney, 71
Jones, Bill, 69
Jones, Sarah Polk, 47
Kentucky, 61
King's Daughters Hospital, **32**
Kinser, R. J., 91–93
Lancaster, England, 53
Langford, J. T., 70
Langford, Mary (Mrs. Absolom
    Thompson), 70
Lebanon, Tenn., 65
Lewisburg, Tenn., 127
Lexington, Ky., 56, 119
Lex Watson Miniature Mules, 144. *See
    also* Watson, Lex
Livestock Day, 142
Louisiana, 47–48, 65
Louisville, Ky., 62
Louisville & Nashville Railroad
    Company (L & N), 7, 23. 27
Lyric Theatre, 24
Madison, Dolly Payne, 53
Madison, James, 73
Madison Square Garden, 128
Manor Hall, **75**
Marion, Francis "Swamp Fox," 65
"Marse" Henry. **See** Watterson, Henry
Martin, Mrs., 63–64
Martin, George W., 54
Martin, Hugh, 59
Martin, Mary (Mrs. Gideon J. Pillow,
    Jr.), 55
Martin, N. Douglas, 63
Martin, Susan Pillow, 59
Maryland, 72, 149
Maryland Farm, 126
Maury, Abram P., 5

Maury County Courthouse, **28**
Maury County Ice Company, 12
Maury County Tobacco Warehouse, 88, **88, 100**
Maury County Tobacco Warehouse Company, 88
Mayes Home, **78**
McCarthy, Frank L., 90
McCord, Jim, 150
McGavock home, 74
McGaw, John, 123
McKay, A. W., 123
McKissack, Myra Thompson, 71
McKissack, Susan. *See* Cheairs, Susan McKissack
Mecklenburgh County, Va., 61
Mecklenburg Declaration of Independence, 43
Melrose, 54
Memphis, Tenn., 56
Mercer Hall, 54, **55**
Mexican War, 55, 72
Muscle Shoals, Ala., 7
Middle Tennessee, 3, 21, 43, 59, 61, 92, 94, 142
Middle Tennessee Packing Company, 14
Mississippi, 57
Missouri, 92
Monsanto Chemical Company, 9–10, **18–19**
Moore, John Trotwood, 73
Mooresville Pike, 67, 69
Morris, Doc, 69
Morristown, Ill., 123
Mt. Olivet Cemetery, 54
Mt. Pleasant, Tenn., 8, 50, 88
Mt. Pleasant Highway, 44, 50, 55, 58, 65
Mt. Vernon, 139–40, 169
Mule Day, **22–23, 30–31, 105, 106,** 142, 144, **145, 147–48,** 150–52; Centennial Celebration, **147;** Championship Mule Stake, 151; Circus, **148,** 150–01; Dance (Ball), 144, 150, 152; Parade, **29, 156, 160–62, 164–65;** Queen, 150; Trot, 152
Musser, Karl, 89

Myra Thompson Home, **62**
Nashville, Chattanooga & St. Louis Railway, 8, 23
Nashville, Florence & Sheffield Division (L & N), 7
Nashville, Tenn., 21, 45, 48, 51, 52–54, 62, 74, 142
Nathaniel Cheairs Place. *See* Cheairs Place
National Carbon Company, 11–12
National Dairy Show, 90, 103
Natchez, Miss., 67–68
New Orleans, La., 45, 53, 62
New York City, 64, 128
Nickajack, 53
North Carolina, 46–47, 51, 72
Oakwood Hall, 52. *See also* Rattle and Snap
Ohio, 149
Old Catholic Church, **35**
Old Hickory. *See* Jackson, Andrew
Orr, Gilbert M., **130**
Orr, Gillie Mac, **107**
Otey, Bishop James Hervey, 25, 48, 50, 54
Paris, Ky., 67
Parks, Raymond, 65
Payne, Anne Fleming (Mrs. Josiah, Sr.), 53
Payne, Anne (Mrs. Gideon Pillow Sr.), 53–55, 57, 59–60
Payne, George, 53
Payne, Josiah, Sr., 53
Payne, Josiah, Jr., 53
Payne, Lucy (Mrs. George Washington Steptoe), 53
Payne, Mary Barnett (Mrs. Joshiah, Jr.), 53
Payne, Mary Woodson (Mrs. George), 53
Payne, Narcissa, 53
Payne, Robert, 53
Payne, William, 53
Pearl Harbor, 151
Philadelphia, Pa., 68
Pine Mountain, 50
Pillow, Abner, 53
Pillow, Alice, 55
Pillow, Amanda (daughter of Gideon and Anne Payne Pillow), 53–54

Pillow, Amanda (daughter of Gideon and Mary Martin Pillow Jr.), 55
Pillow, Anne Payne. *See* Payne, Anne
Pillow, Annie, 55
Pillow, Cynthia (Mrs. John E. Saunders), 53–54
Pillow, Cynthia Saunders (Mrs. William Decatur Bethel), 57
Pillow, Edward Dale, 57
Pillow, Elvira Dale, 57
Pillow, Fanny, 57
Pillow, George, 55
Pillow, Gertrude, 55
Pillow, Gideon, Sr., 53–55, 57–60, 65
Pillow, Gideon J., Jr., 53, 55–57
Pillow, Gideon, III, 55
Pillow, Granville, 53, 59
Pillow, Granville, Jr., 59
Pillow, Jasper, Sr., 53
Pillow, Jerome Bonaparte, 53, 57–58
Pillow, Jerome Bonaparte, Jr., 57
Pillow, John (father), 53
Pillow, John (son), 53
Pillow, Lizzie, 55
Pillow, Martha Woodson, 57
Pillow, Mordecai, 53
Pillow, Narcissa, 55
Pillow, Robert Martin, 55
Pillow, Sallie Polk, 55, 57
Pillow, William (son of Granville), 59
Pillow, William (son of Jasper, Sr.), 53
Pillow, William (son of John), 53
Pillow Park, **148**
Pillow Place, 59–60
Pittsburgh, Pa., 126–27
Polk, Andrew, 48–49
Polk, Antoinette, 48–49
Polk, George, 44, 50–51
Polk, Hamilton, 44
Polk, James Knox, 6, 24, 47
Polk, Bishop Leonidas, 25, 44, 47–48, 50
Polk, Lucius, 44–47, 49
Polk, Rufus, 44
Polk, William (father), 43–46, 50–51

Polk, William (son), 44, 48
Polk Estate, 43
Prestwould, 61
Princess Theatre, 24, **24**
Pulaski Pike, 69
Queens County, Md., 72
Raleigh, N.C., 43
Rattle and Snap, 44, 50–52, **51.** *See also* Oakwood Hall
Reverend Frederic Augustus Thompson House and Garden, 62. *See also* Thompson, Rev. Frederic Augustus
Richmond County, N.C., 72
Ridley, Anne Lewis Pillow, 57
Ridley, Annie Gray (Mrs. William Parker Halliday), 56
Ridley, Campbell Pillow, 56
Ridley, Eunice Holderness, 56
Ridley, Eva Campbell James (Mrs. Charles Worthington Jewell), 56
Ridley, Evelyn Shapard, 56–57
Ridley, James Webb Smith, 57, 60
Ridley, Mary, 55, 57
Ridley, Sarah Ann, 56, 152
Ridley, William P., 55–57, 66
Ridley, William P., II, 56
Ridley Farm, 45, **116**
Roach, Ann, **155**
Robertson, James, 52, 54
Rogers, Will, 144
Roscher, Eleanor, 152
Rush, Abigail Ferrell, 73
Rush, Sarah (Mrs. Nathaniel Cheairs III), 73
Rush, William, 73
Rutherford County, Tenn., 44
Samuel Mayes Home. *See* Mayes Home
Sanford, Mary Brown (Mrs. Absolom Thompson), 70–71
San Francisco, Calif., 90
Santa Fe, Tenn., 8
Saunders, Cynthia Pillow, 54
Saunders, John E. 54
Saunders, John Edward, 54
Saunders, Narcissa Saunders, 54

Scales, Louise, 152
Schofield, John, 74
Shapard, Van, 152
Shelbyville, Tenn., 90, 128, **130**
Shenandoah Valley, Va., 68
Skipwith, Peyton, 60
Skipwith Place, 60, **60**, 61–62
Sloan, Martha Stratton, 152
Smiser, Ellen (Mrs. James Gray Booker), 68
Smiser, John, 67–68
Southern Bell Telephone Company, 8
South Park, Pittsburgh, 126
South Park Matinee Club, 126
Southport, Tenn., 8
Spain, 61, 146
Spring Hill, Tenn., 8, 43, **62**, 63–65, 69–74, **72, 90**, 126
St. Dominic's Catholic Church, **35**
Steptoe, George Washington, 53
St. John's Episcopal Church, 44, **49**, 50–51, 54, 74
St. Louis World's Fair, 66
Stowe, Harriet Beecher, 63
St. Peter's Episcopal Church, **37**, 50
Strahl, Otho, 74
Sweeney, Sam, Sr., 58
Sweeney, Sam, Jr., 58–59
Switzerland, 49
TEPCO, 22
Tennessee Knitting Mills, **15–16**
Tennessee River, 54
Tennessee Valley Authority (TVA), 4, 10, 21–24, 26, 28, 147
Tennessee Walking Horse, 5, **6**, 24, 119–21, 126–28, 144

Tennessee Walking Horse Breeders' Association of America, 127–28
Tennessee Walking Horse National Celebration, 90, 128, **130–31**
Texas, 66, 167
Thomas, Edward, 60
Thomas, Mrs. Edward, 60
Thomas, Smith, 123
Thompson, Absolom, 69–70, 74
Thompson, Andrew, 70
Thompson, Fred, 71
Thompson, Rev. Frederic Augustus, 62–64, 70. *See also* Reverend Frederic Augustus Thompson House and Garden
Thompson, Hattie Cheairs (Mrs. N. Douglas Martin), 71
Thompson, James (father), 63, 69–70
Thompson, James (son), 70
Thompson, James Turner Sanford, 71
Thompson, John, 70
Thompson, Leo, 72
Thompson, Martha Wilson, 66
Thompson, Matthew, 70
Thompson, Mayes, 71
Thompson, Minnie, 71
Thompson, Myra, 62–65. *See also* Myra Thompson Home
Thompson, Sarah Myra Holland, 62
Thompson, St. Clair, 71
Thompson, Susie Pointer, 71
Thompson Place, 69, **69**, 71–72
Thompson Station, Tenn., 63
Tolley, Joe, 123
Trans Crossing, Tenn., 22
Treasure Island, Calif., 90

Turney, Mary Evie, 67–68
Turney, Robert R., 68
United States Military Academy, 25
United States Naval Academy, 25
United States War Department, 27
University of the South at Sewanee, 48
USDA (United States Department of Agriculture), 88, 140
Van Buren, Martin, 47
Van Leer, Rebecca (Mrs. Andrew Polk), 48
Victor Chemical Works, 9–10, **10**
Vine Hill, 54
Vinson, Mary (Mrs. Granville Pillow Jr.), 59
Virginia, 6, 53, 70, 119, 139
Virginia House of Burgesses, 53
Virginia Order of Cincinatti, 53
Voss, Ronald, 72
Voss, Mrs. Ronald, 72
Walkaway Farms, 127
War between the States. *See* Civil War
Ward, J. Truman, 126
Warfield Place, **81**
War of 1812, 5, 45
Washington, D.C., 46, 54, 72, 88
Washington, George 139–40, 147
Washington (state), 90
Watson, Lex, 69, 107, 144, 146, 149–50. *See also* Lex Watson Miniature Mules
Watterson, Harvey, 64
Webster, Garfield, **85**
Webster, W. J., Jr., 123
West Brook, 44
Western Union, 8

West Point, 26, 47
West Tennessee, 72
Wheeler Dam, **17**, 26
White House, the, 45–46
Whitfield, John, 74
Whitfield, Mrs. John, 74
Williams, H. Melville, 57
Williams, Robert M., 123
Williams, Sallie Polk Pillow. *See* Pillow, Sallie Polk
Williamson Camp. *See* George Williamson Camp
Willamson County, Tenn., 5, 53, 61,65, 68, 73
Williamsport, Tenn., 8
Williamsport Pike, 60, **60**
Will's Grove, 43, 46
Wilson, Flavel, 66
Wilson, John, 66
Wilson, Leonora, 66
Wilson, Robert, 65–67
Wilson, William, 66
Wilson Dam, 7, 26
Wilson Place, 65, **65**, 66–67
W. M. Dean Marble Company, **9**
Woldridge, W. P., 123
W. P. Ridley farm. *See* Ridley farm
Yeatman, Mr., 45
Yeatman, Mrs. 45
Yeatman, Harry, 47
Yeatman, James, 47
Yeatman, Jenny, 45
Yeatman Farm, 45
Yorktown, Va., 53
Zion Cemetery, 66
Zion Presbyterian Church, 66